Saints Alive – Claiming The Saints For Protestant Preaching

Alex A. Gondola, Jr.

CSS Publishing Company, Inc.
Lima, Ohio

SAINTS ALIVE — CLAIMING THE SAINTS
FOR PROTESTANT PREACHING

FIRST EDITION
Copyright © 2017
by CSS Publishing Co., Inc.

Published by CSS Publishing Company, Inc., Lima, Ohio 45807. All rights reserved. No part of this publication may be reproduced in any manner whatsoever without the prior permission of the publisher, except in the case of brief quotations embodied in critical articles and reviews. Inquiries should be addressed to: CSS Publishing Company, Inc., Permissions Department, 5450 N. Dixie Highway, Lima, Ohio 45807.

Library of Congress Cataloging-in-Publication Data

Names: Gondola, Alex A., author.
Title: Saints alive : claiming the saints for Protestant preaching / Alex A. Gondola, Jr.
Description: FIRST EDITION . | Lima, Ohio : CSS Publishing Company, Inc., 2017. | Includes bibliographical references and index.
Identifiers: LCCN 2017027448 (print) | LCCN 2017036284 (ebook) | ISBN 9780788028458 (eBook) | ISBN 0788028456 (eBook) | ISBN 9780788028441 (pbk. : alk. paper) | ISBN 0788028448 (pbk. : alk. paper)
Subjects: LCSH: Preaching. | Christian saints.
Classification: LCC BV4211.3 (ebook) | LCC BV4211.3 .G66 2017 (print) | DDC 270.092/2--dc23

For more information about CSS Publishing Company resources, visit our website at www.csspub.com, email us at csr@csspub.com, or call (800) 241-4056.

e-book:
ISBN-13: 978-0-7880-2845-8
ISBN-10: 0-7880-2845-6

ISBN-13: 978-0-7880-2844-1
ISBN-10: 0-7880-2844-8

PRINTED IN USA

Contents

Preface 5
Augustine of Hippo: "Sinner And Saint" 7
Hildegard of Bingen: "A Feather On The Breath Of God" 15
St. Patrick: "Christ In All Things" 23
Francis of Assisi: "Knight Of Christ" 31
Elizabeth Seton: "Saintly Mother" 37
Thomas Aquinas: "The Angelic Doctor" 43
Kateri Tekakwitha: "Lily of the Mohawks" 51
Father Damien: "Contagious Faith" 59
Katharine Drexel: "Poor Little Rich Girl" 67
Mother Teresa: "Saint Of The Gutters" 75
Nicholas of Myra: "An Advent Saint" 83
You and I: "Called To Be Saints" 91

Preface

During my last pastorate I lived 25 miles from the unincorporated community of Maria Stein, Ohio. This tiny settlement is in a farming region, graced by mile after mile of green, swaying soybeans or corn, gentle rolling hills, and narrow country roads. There would seem to be little in Maria Stein to draw a crowd. But surprisingly, around 20,000 visitors make their way there annually. They are mostly Roman Catholics making pilgrimages to The National Shrine of the Holy Relics, the second largest collection of relics in America, set in a former convent on a hill. Around 1,000 relics of saints are reverently displayed there.

The spiritual power of Maria Stein was evident even to me, a Protestant, and I visited that peaceful setting often. The devotion with which my Roman Catholic brothers and sisters approached the relics — some women dressed modestly in long skirts and head scarves, both men and women fervently praying their rosaries — was moving to me. Still, I also had to admit that I didn't quite "get it." What is behind what Roman Catholics refer to as "the cult of veneration of the saints?" (Please note: while the word "cult" has some ominous meanings, here it simply means "adoration" in Latin). Could there also be spiritual enrichment for me, a Protestant, in focusing on the saints?

I felt I could benefit by learning more about some of the historical figures who have been elevated to sainthood. As I studied their life stories, I also came to realize the saints might be a fruitful topic for Protestant preaching. Biographies, after all, are among the best sellers every year, and biographical movies like

The Theory of Everything or *Unbroken* are wildly popular. Most of us learn a lot by studying other people's lives. In fact, by studying biographies, we learn about ourselves. Other's stories challenge us to wonder, "How might I have felt in that situation?" Or, "How would I have reacted?" One year, while senior pastor at St. Paul United Church of Christ in Wapakoneta, Ohio, I preached on one saint a month. That series is the basis for this book.

For the most part these twelve saints are presented with the oldest first. This provides a chronological survey of saints throughout church history. However, I depart from this pattern slightly in May and significantly in December. In May, Elizabeth Seton, a "later" saint, is my topic for Mother's Day, while Saint Nicholas, an "early" saint, is preached on in Advent. The two saints' connections with these holidays are obvious.

This slim volume is offered as an aide to sermon preparation, and/or a source for devotional reading and/or as a resource for youth group or adult study programs. I hope it will increase an appreciation of the saints and for their witness among my fellow Protestants. Roman Catholic readers might be interested in how one Protestant preacher approached sermons on "their" saints. Actually, they should be "our" saints, because these Spirit-led, faithful, inspiring and challenging believers are treasures not only for Roman Catholicism, but for the entire church. As such, they rightly deserve our adoration, here defined not as "worship" but as "deep love and respect."

Saints Alive – Augustine of Hippo: "Sinner And Saint"

Romans 13: 11-14

One Sunday a Christian education director had the children make a gigantic, "World-wide Web." It was like a spider's web made of many strands of colored yarn. Each child traced and cut out a cardboard figure representing himself or herself, and hung it on the web. It was a reminder to the children of how we are interconnected: with each other and with Christians around the world.

We are connected, "upward" to God, outward to other people and the rest of creation, and backward in time. The church has long spoken of "The Communion of Saints." That's the belief that those who died in Christ are still with us in spirit. As Hebrews puts it, they surround us like a "great cloud of witnesses" (12:1, NRSV). Certainly our understanding of the faith and the church has been shaped by great figures from the past.

I'd like to speak about one great saint this morning. When I read the scripture lesson from Romans 13, I thought of him. He's Saint Augustine. He was bishop of Hippo in Africa around 400 AD. Even though Augustine lived long ago and far away, he has influenced the way we think about our faith, the Church, and even about ourselves. Some scholars believe that, after the writers of the Bible, Augustine was the most influential Christian who ever lived. I think it's worthwhile being reintroduced to this intriguing and controversial character, Augustine of Hippo: sinner and saint, for we are connected to him.

Augustine was born in North Africa, in what is presently Algeria, in 354 AD.[1] Christianity had only been the official religion of the Roman Empire for about forty years. So, many of the people were still pagan, including Augustine's father, Patrick, who was a minor Roman official. His mother Monica however, was a Christian, and very devout.

Augustine was raised in what we might call the "Bible Belt" of the Roman Empire. I once heard North Africa in the fourth century compared to "Bible-quoting, Bible-toting Arkansas" (not that there's anything wrong with Arkansas). Today we might label many of the North African Christians "fundamentalists." Augustine had a brilliant, steel-trap mind. Like some people today who have been raised in the church, Augustine felt he had outgrown his childhood faith and drifted away.

He went off to school and studied rhetoric: argumentation and debate. Rhetoric was a stepping stone to high public office, which was what Augustine sought. But he began his career by establishing his own school, using a wealthy patron's money. Within two years Augustine was well known throughout his region as a brilliant and popular teacher of argumentation and debate.

When he was just sixteen, Augustine took a concubine. He lived with her for fifteen years. They never married but had a son. For nine years Augustine, the

---

1 Phillip Cary, *Augustine: Philosopher and Saint* (Chantilly, VA: The Teaching Company Great Courses no. 611, 1997). This well-produced and engaging series of videotaped lectures provides an excellent introduction to Augustine's life and thought.

dropout Christian, was a Manichean. Manichaenism was a heresy that combined Christian ideas with Persian religion.

Augustine's lifestyle and his beliefs drove his mother Monica crazy. But, like many other loving and devout parents, she kept praying for her child's soul. She once went to her local priest and wept for Augustine. The priest comforted Monica by saying, "The son of these tears cannot perish." We should never discount the power of a loving parent's tears.

Augustine eventually moved to Milan, then the capitol of the Roman Empire, to get closer to the action. Remember, what he ultimately wanted was a political career. He came in contact with Ambrose, the bishop of Milan. Ambrose was a pagan turned Christian who was both brilliant and courageous. He once blocked the door to the local cathedral to keep the Roman emperor out, until the emperor confessed his guilt and repented for something terrible he'd done. Ambrose, representing the church, challenged the power of the Roman empire, and the Roman emperor backed down!

Ambrose showed Augustine it was intellectually respectable to be a Christian. Augustine began to struggle with leaving Manichaenism and returning to his childhood faith. He was very honest about his struggles in his famous work *Confessions*. One thing Augustine didn't want to give up was his relationship with his concubine. Augustine wasn't wildly promiscuous, but he had lived with this woman for fifteen years. While he would never marry her, he didn't relish the thought losing her company, either. "I was in love with loving," Augustine confessed. So he prayed his well-known, half-hearted prayer, "God, give me chastity and continence, but not yet!"

Over several months Augustine stumbled back toward Christianity. One day he tore his hair, pounded his chest, and wept in agony, "How long, O God, how long? How long before you release me from my sins and tears?" Instantly Augustine heard above the garden wall the voice of an unseen child singing, "Take up and read, take up and read," as if the child were playing a game with a friend. Augustine couldn't think of a childhood game that used those words. He believed the child's voice as a message for him.

Augustine rushed to another part of the garden where he had left some writings by the apostle Paul. He picked up the book, resolved to follow the first words, and opened it. His eyes immediately fell on verses from the epistle lesson assigned for this Sunday:

"Let us live honorably...not in reveling and drunkenness, not in debauchery and licentiousness, not in quarreling and jealousy. Instead put on the Lord Jesus Christ, and make no provision for the flesh, to gratify its desires" (Romans 13:13-14, NRSV).

Augustine read no further. He didn't need to, for the scripture passage seemed directed at him: no more licentious living. Augustine immediately went inside and told his mother he wanted to become a Christian. Monica leapt for joy. Not too long after Ambrose, the bishop, baptized him.

Augustine left Milan to found and oversee the first monastery in North Africa. All he wanted was to pray quietly, enjoy God's presence, think and write. But against his will, local church leaders dragged him into sanctuary and ordained him a priest, and later a bishop. Augustine spent the last forty years of his life serving the church.

This he did brilliantly. Augustine would pace the floor restlessly, dictating to rotating teams of stenographers while another team of copyists reproduced his books, letters, and sermons and mailed them off. He wrote more than 100 books and wrote and preached 8,000 sermons, leading worship nearly every consecutive day for forty years.

Because Augustine wrote so much, so early and so well, his thinking has influenced the church for 1,600 years. Some of Augustine's ideas, like his "Just War Theory", are turned to today. Other things he wrote have caused a lot of pain: like his notion that babies come into the world with original sin clinging to them, which had to be washed off in baptism. If it wasn't washed off, and they died without being baptized, they went to Limbo, Augustine believed, this and many in the church with him for hundreds of years. The doctrine of predestination, the idea that some are born for salvation and some for damnation, and our fate can never be changed, an idea he perfected, has also caused a lot of pain.

But I don't think we need to dwell on what some have called the "shadow side" of Augustine. I'd like to mention three things he did have really blessed the world. For one thing, Augustine was the first writer we know of anywhere really to share his inner life in depth. His *Confessions* are the first great surviving autobiography from *anywhere* in the world. He wrote them after he had been a bishop for many years. But in spite of his revered position he was completely honest about his thoughts, feelings, fears, losses, grief, and sins. Augustine dared to let himself be known to encourage others in their walk of faith.

In so doing he gives dignity to our souls and to our inner struggles. He blesses the long journey that many of us take, with its frequent ups and downs, twists and turns, false starts and setbacks that draw us, hopefully, ever nearer to God. Augustine was the first great interpreter and champion of the inner life, the idea that unless we get things right on the inside, things will never be right on the outside. Or as he put it, our hearts will be restless until they find their rest in God.

Secondly, Augustine was a great systematic theologian. He has influenced how we think about the sacraments, the church and God. He was one of the first Christian writers to struggle with the doctrine of the Trinity, for example, and the very first person known to talk about "God in three persons," a phrase we use every Sunday in the Gloria Patri.[2]

Augustine didn't always think he got things right. He once was walking along the beach, taking a break from writing about the Trinity. At the beach he saw a boy running back and forth from the ocean carrying water in a shell. The boy stopped and poured the water into a hole in the sand. "What are you doing?" Augustine asked him. "I'm trying to put the ocean in the hole," the boy answered.

Augustine realized he was trying to do the same thing, trying to capture the divine mystery of the Trinity into his all-too-small mind. But he kept on trying, even though Augustine knew, as he put it, that when, "We are talking about God, what wonder is it that we do not understand? If we did understand, then it is not

---

2   Phillip Cary, *The History of Christian Theology* (Chantilly, VA: The Teaching Company Great Courses no. 6450, 2008). Part I, Lecture 10 describes at greater length Augustine's contributions to this central Christian doctrine.

God." His thinking on the sacraments, God and the Trinity have shaped the church ever since.

Thirdly, Augustine has left us with the example of a believer who, starting from his conversion at least, always took God and God's word seriously. From that dramatic day, when he picked up the book in his garden, and read, Augustine devoted himself body, mind, and spirit, to knowing and following God.

He wrote, with a sense of wistfulness, "Too late I loved you, O Beauty ever ancient and ever new! Too late I loved you! And behold, you were within me... and there I searched for you." But Augustine's life, with its many accomplishments, shows us it is never too late for any of us to turn back to God — and that God will use and bless whatever time we have left after we make that turning.

Saint Augustine died at age 75 in the year 430 CE, in the city of Hippo, while the vandals were attacking just outside the gates. He died surrounded by scriptures, written at his request by friends in large letters and hung on the walls, where his failing eyes could see them constantly.

But his words and his example influence us still. The life of this saint reminds us to take our inner lives and our relationship with God seriously, and that our real joy comes from our relationship with God.

Saints Alive – Hildegard of Bingen: "A Feather On The Breath Of God"

Psalm 150

How many of you are familiar with Hildegard of Bingen? Please raise your hand if you know that name. There's a few hands, maybe ten percent of our congregation. Good! This morning I have the opportunity, and privilege, to introduce you to one of the most remarkable Christians ever. I hope to bring this long-dead saint "alive."

Hildegard was a mystic. She had powerful, direct encounters with God. She wrote beautiful, soaring plain songs — some of which we heard in our gathering music. Her compositions lift the spirit. But Hildegard was firmly grounded. She was skilled administrator, author, preacher, scientist, healer, art sponsor, playwright, and adviser to popes and kings. She even has been called the first food writer of the Western world! Hildegard was a genius, gifted in many things. You might call her a "Renaissance woman." Except she lived some three hundred years before the Renaissance began. Hildegard was born into a noble family in Germany in 1098. She was put into the care of the Roman Catholic Church early. Hildegard was the tenth and last child. Her pious parents "tithed" her. They gave her over to religious life. She was a "thank you" to God for the nine other children who came first. At age eight she became the ward of an older nun, who gave her a minimal education. At age fourteen, she joined the convent herself.

Technically speaking, Hildegard is not a "saint." Rather, her official Roman Catholic designation is "blessed," since no miracles have been attributed to her. Nevertheless, Hildegard is celebrated with a feast day, September 17, and many around the world consider her example "saintly."

She was a sickly child, given to illness her whole life long. Once, as a young adult, she was paralyzed for a time. Reading her diaries, some believe Hildegard suffered from migraines. These may have been connected to the visions she received, starting at age three and continuing until she died.

She described one vision like this: "And the image I saw spoke: I, the highest blazing power, enkindle all sparks of life. I breathe forth nothing deadly. With my wings I fly around the circle of the earth. I blaze above the beauty of the field, shine in the waters, and burn in the sun, the moon and the stars. I, the fiery power, remain hidden in all these things; they burn in me. For I am life." Hildegard saw God as a blazing fire.

Though she received visions of God, or messages from God, Hildegard was humble. Writing about another vision, she described herself like this:

"Listen: there was once a king sitting on his throne. Around him stood great and wonderfully beautiful columns ornamented with ivory, bearing the banners of the king with great honor. Then it pleased the king to raise a small feather from the ground and he commanded it to fly. The feather flew, not because of anything in itself but because the air bore it along. Thus I am...a feather on the breath of God." She thought of herself as light as a feather, not "weighty" and called herself "untaught" and "unlearned."

For half her life, Hildegard kept her visions secret. She perhaps was afraid people would think she was insane. But at age 42 she became severely ill, again. Hildegard interpreted this as God's punishment for bottling up her visions. She told a priest what was going on. He encouraged her to write her visions down. They became the basis for the first of the nine books she wrote, *Scrivas*, which, in Latin means "know the ways of the Lord." After she started writing, she got better. This made Hildegard think sharing her visions was God's will.

This is not to say she wasn't already busy with God's work. The nuns recognized her abilities early. By this point she was in charge of a large convent, elected by the other sisters. During her career she established two new convents, raising the funds herself. This was remarkable in an era when women rarely conducted business. Most were not even allowed to own property.

In those days, convents served as hospices and hospitals. Hildegard became knowledgeable in the healing arts, especially dermatology, where she's considered the first expert ever. She studied botany intensively to understand the medicinal properties of plants, and put her learning into books. She was the first female botanist recorded anywhere. She additionally wrote about the characteristics of foods and herbs. Today she might be called a "natural healer."

Because she lived close to nature, Hildegard was an advocate for the environment. She wrote, "Who... trusts God will also honor the existing world, the course of sun and moon, the winds and air, the earth and water, everything...God created for the glory of human beings and for their protection. Human beings have no other ground to stand on. If they abandon this world, it will result in destruction by demons..." That's a good message for today as we face environmental challenges.

She took careful notes on what made patients better, and wrote medical texts. She advocated better hygiene, and installed running water and sewers in the two convents she built. Hildegard's influence spread far beyond the walls of her convent. At age seventy she began the first of four preaching missions. Traveling through Germany and France, she brought the good news to common people, particularly preaching repentance. It was almost unheard of for a woman, especially an elderly nun, to preach in public, let alone travel widely and address huge congregations. But Hildegard's fame was such she drew big crowds.

She was a composer, even with no formal musical training. She wrote some eighty songs and produced the first known Passion Play. The music of the church in those days was Gregorian chant, called plainsong because it was plain: simple, monophonic, usually sung without instruments. But Hildegard's songs were different. The common Gregorian chant had a range of less than an octave. Hildegard's vocal lines covered two octaves, or more. She encouraged the sisters to stretch themselves praising God. Her music is praised today for its lovely, ethereal quality.

She not only was an artist herself. She inspired artistry in others. Some of the most beautiful illuminated manuscripts of the Middle Ages were created by nuns in her convent to illustrate her books. Some scholars think Hildegard designed them herself, and supervised their production. In any history of women artists, she almost always is mentioned. Hildegard even invented her own alphabet to help her nuns, many of whom were illiterate, to communicate with each other.

By the end of her life (and she lived to be 81, fooling everyone who thought she'd die young) Hildegard was famous. Popes, bishops and kings sought her advice. Sometimes the rich and powerful got her opinions, whether they wanted them or not.

For example, she wrote to the Holy Roman Emperor, Frederick the First: "O King, it is of utmost necessity that you take care how you act. In the mysterious vision, I see you acting like a child. You live an insane, absurd life before God. There still is time." In other words, "shape up!"

The Emperor never wrote back. But Hildegard kept after him. It was unprecedented in the twelfth century for a nun to challenge the Holy Roman Emperor and call him to task. One commentator called this an example of "social justice."

Hildegard took other stands that landed her in trouble. Near the end of her life she nursed a nobleman with a notorious reputation. As she came to know him she was convinced he was repentant and intended to change. Unfortunately he died soon after. She allowed the nobleman to be buried in a cemetery at her convent: sacred ground. But the local bishop wouldn't have it. He had excommunicated the man, and wasn't about to allow him a Christian burial. He ordered the body dug up, and removed.

When Hildegard objected, the bishop censured her. He forbade all singing at her convent, and denied the nuns Communion. This was harsh. You can imagine how important music was to Hildegard, being a composer. No communion meant no daily connection with the Body of Christ. Plus, if one of the nuns died, she would face judgment without her sins forgiven. Their souls and future salvation were at stake.

This interdict went on for about a year, while Hildegard protested vigorously, right up to the pope. Finally the ban was lifted, the nobleman reburied in church ground and full worship restored. Sadly, Hildegard died a few months later. Her defense of the repentant nobleman has been called her final act of social justice.

That's a short account of the long life of Hildegard of Bingen. She's been labeled an early feminist, an environmentalist, a female genius, a pioneer of the spirit — and one of the most important people to live between 500 and 1,500.

Still, this remarkable figure largely was forgotten, until around 1850. At that time her grave was dug up and she was re-interred. Nuns from her convent began translating her works and bringing them public attention. Today this once overlooked nun is known worldwide. A CD of her Gregorian chants, *Canticles of Ecstasy*, is a best-seller.

But, what does this long-dead visionary have to say to us? In what way is this saint "alive" today? I think her example is instructive on several levels. For one, Hildegard is a good illustration of keeping on keeping on, in the face of trouble. Think about her life: separated from her parents and siblings at age eight, physically ill much of the time, alternately accepted and rejected by the church she loved. Yet through it all, Hildegard both kept the faith and shared it. Remember the international preaching missions she started at seventy?

Hildegard also reminds us we shouldn't — and often can't — neglect or reject our calling. It took half her life for her to accept her visions, and share them with others. As a woman, largely uneducated, she had little standing in Medieval society. She thought herself nothing more than a feather on the breath of God. But God wanted to use her. God often chooses to use those the world rejects. Saint Paul put it like this: "...God chose what is foolish in the world to shame the wise; God chose what is weak in the world to shame the strong; low and despised in the world, things that are not to reduce to nothing things that are so that no one might boast in the presence of God" (1 Corinthians 1.27-29, NRSV).

Hildegard had a calling. So do you and I. Let's not think too little of ourselves. God wants to use us to advance God's kingdom. Maybe astonishing things will get accomplished through us, when we embrace and live our calling, as Hildegard did.

Finally, Hildegard provides us with a wonderful example of joy in worship. As one commentator put it, "(She) was not one of those Christians who concentrated so hard on being miserable sinners that they wanted to eat worms." In an era when nuns commonly dressed modestly, often in black, the sisters in Hildegard's convents wore lavish silk habits with golden headpieces and veils in bright colors. Some wore crosses with jewels.

Why? Because they were the brides of Christ, and Christ deserved a bride to be her most beautiful. From her ecstatic visions to the songs she wrote to the stunning manuscripts she commissioned to her elaborate nun's habits, Hildegard promoted a religion of joy. So also, we believers are called to be joyful, as in Philippians 4:4, where Paul commands, "Rejoice in the Lord always; again I will say, Rejoice" (RSV). Let's thank God, and praise God, for the good news of our salvation, and spread that good news around.

Victoria Sirota, a distinguished church musician and Episcopalian priest, has said, "If you know God, you know Hildegard." That is, something of the creativity and goodness of God shone through her. I can think of no better way of closing than to quote her:

"Be a wind, helping those in need.
Be a dew, consoling the abandoned.
Be the rain-soaked air, giving heart to the weary.
Filling their hunger with instruction
By giving them your soul."

That's good advice from a saint who actually lived it!

Saints Alive – St. Patrick: "Christ In All Things"

Philippians 3:10-14

On this Sunday near Saint Patrick's Day, I'd like to begin the sermon with an Irish greeting: *"Cead Mile Failta,"*("Keed Mila Felt-ya"). That's my best Irish for "A hundred thousand welcomes," which, I am told, is the appropriate way to greet any assembly (whether there happen to be 100,000 people or 100). As you might have guessed, I'm *not* Irish myself. Still, on Saint Patrick's Day, many of us like to be at least a little bit "Irish." I once read a newspaper article listing ten things anyone could do to be authentically Irish on Saint Patrick's Day. The article went something like this:

1. Drink a pot of tea.
2. Start *Ulysses* by James Joyce (notice it suggests we "start *Ulysses,*" but doesn't require that we finish it).
3. 3. Go to your local video store and rent *The Field*, *In the Name of the Father*, *The Secret of Roan Inish*, or perhaps *The Quiet Man*.
4. Walk in the rain.
5. Tell/listen to a long story.
6. Listen to the Pogues, IJ-2,The Dubliners, The Cranberries or Dropkick Murphy's (for those of us not rock fans, those are apparently Irish rock bands).

7. Respect the spirits, fairies, and the leprechauns that populate the earth.
8. Drink another pot of tea.
9. Wear green (in the 1790's Irishmen were imprisoned by the British for wearing green).
10. (And) "Laugh heartily, philosophize gently, and carry on bravely in the face of adversity."[3]

To that list of wonderful things we can all do today to be more "Irish," I would add one more: "Listen to a sermon about Saint Patrick!" That's what we're going to do today! Who was Saint Patrick? I mean, really. What did he stand for? I think the life of Saint Patrick has a lot to teach us: about overcoming tragedy, about listening to God, about humility, about self-sacrifice, about finding Christ in all things. These are all good things to remember always, especially during Lent. Let me then share with you the story of Saint Patrick, as I learned it.

Patrick was born not in Ireland but in Britain (that's ironic, isn't it: that Saint Patrick, the patron saint of Ireland was actually British?) in the early years of the church, around 390 AD.[4] Britain was then considered the outermost colony of the Roman empire, at the edge of the civilized world. Remember Hadrian's Wall, built to keep those "barbarian" Scotsmen out? Patrick himself was of noble birth. His father was a public official. His family had a villa, land, servants, and slaves and Patrick enjoyed an easy life.

That is, until he was sixteen years old, when his part of the countryside was attacked by Irish raiders.

---

[3] Adapted from *Union News*, Springfield, Massachusetts, March 16, 1994.

[4] A & E Home Video, *Biography of St. Patrick* (VHS, 2000) and SHANACHIE Studio, *St. Patrick, The Irish Legend*, d. Robert Hughes (DVD, 2000) are informative dramatizations of Patrick's life and times. Both can be found online.

These fierce warriors sailed across the Irish Sea in animal-skin boats. When they landed they burned villages, plundered estates, and captured slaves. Along with thousands of his countrymen, Patrick was taken back to Ireland. For the next six years he was a slave, mostly herding pigs.

Patrick had not been especially religious, although his father was a deacon in the Christian Church, and his grandfather a priest (at a time when priests could still marry). But during this period of suffering his faith grew stronger. In his autobiography, titled *Confessions*, which he wrote late in life, Patrick reported that he prayed "One hundred times a day, as many at night." Patrick continues, "Even when I was staying out in the woods or on the mountain . . . I used to feel no ill effect. . ." Patrick was developing a relationship with God through prayer, a relationship that would last the rest of his life.

At many points in his life, Patrick had visions. In his autobiography he writes that many messages came to him in dreams. For example, after he had been a slave for six years, one night in his sleep he heard a voice saying, "You have been right to fast because you will soon return to your home." Soon afterward Patrick received another message in a dream which said, "Look, your ship is ready."

Believing in God's promise, Patrick resolved to escape. He walked 200 miles to the southern coast, a runaway slave in danger at every moment of being recaptured and killed. But God kept Patrick safe and he did indeed find a ship: a very strange ship. It was departing Ireland for Britain with a cargo of dogs! The captain originally refused to have anything to do with this tattered fugitive. But the young man prayed and the captain changed his mind. But what a voyage! Escaping Ireland on a ship full of dogs (I'm guessing they were Irish setters)! It was an unusual homecoming. The ship struck land on a desolate part of the coast.

Patrick and the crew, plus the dogs, wandered for 28 days without seeing people, finding a village or getting a decent meal. Patrick survived the ordeal with his faith strengthened. At 22, he decided to become a priest. He studied in France, was ordained and returned to his family in Britain where he lived in peace and happiness for about twenty years.

Then he had another one of his dreams. In the dream a man, representing the Voice of the Irish, spoke to him, saying, "We pray thee, holy youth, come and walk among us once again." Patrick interpreted the dream as a call to service. He set about getting assigned to be a missionary to Ireland.

Now Patrick, mind you, was not a self-promoting sort of person. His autobiography shows us how little he thought of himself. He refers to himself as "Patrick, a sinner, most unlearned, the least of all the faithful... utterly despised by many." Apparently his superiors weren't that impressed with Patrick either, because the assignment to preach to the Irish went to someone else. Only after the first candidate died was Patrick sent to Ireland as his superiors' second choice.

It was no small task. The Celtic people who lived in Ireland were fierce, pagan warriors. There were numerous local chieftains and a class of Druid priests that were threatened by change. Patrick returned to Ireland, where he had been a slave, at the risk of his life. At any moment the kings, the Druids or the common people could have risen up and had him killed. Patrick writes, "Every day I expected either violent death or to be defrauded or to be reduced to slavery." But he also writes, "If I should be worthy, I am ready to give even my life unhesitatingly and most joyfully for his name's sake." Patrick did suffer. There were years of tiring work, frequent threats to his life, hunger, persecution, and even a period of imprisonment, with his legs in irons. Yet patient Patrick stuck with the task.

Danger from his enemies was not his only problem. The greatest disappointment of Patrick's life was his betrayal by a friend. It seems that when Patrick was fifteen, he committed a youthful sin (he doesn't say what) for which he was repentant. Some ten or fifteen years later, before taking holy orders, he confessed that sin to his superior, another priest. Thirty years later that that same man, whom Patrick called "his dearest friend," made Patrick's confession public!

Patrick was humiliated, tried, and removed from office as a Bishop. This betrayal by his friend was even worse than being a slave. But Patrick rallied, appealed his case to Rome, where the ancient sin was forgiven and his bishopric restored.

In the last thirty years of his life, Patrick Christianized most of Ireland. He himself baptized tens of thousands of people. Before his time, there were few Christians in Ireland. They were outnumbered and threatened. Since Patrick, Ireland has become one of the bulwarks of the faith. Ireland was a light to the church in the Dark Ages. British Christians used to send their sons to Ireland to get a good foundation for the Christian life. Even today, 85% of the population of Ireland is Roman Catholic. The Irish still have one of the highest records of church attendance of anywhere in the world. All this because a humble British Christian named Patrick accepted God's calling to bring the gospel to the same people who had made him a slave!

How could we sum up the life of Saint Patrick? There are many admirable characteristics to this man. He didn't give up in the face of suffering, danger, or betrayal. He was faithful in prayer. He responded to the guidance of God. He was humble and sincere and willing to sacrifice himself for others. He was able to forgive even when harmed.

But most of all, he was able to find Christ in all things. That's what his wonderful prayer, "Saint Patrick's Breastplate" is about, Christ in all things. This long prayer ends:

"Christ be with me, Christ within me,
Christ behind me, Christ before me,
Christ beside me, Christ to win me,
Christ to comfort and restore me.
Christ beneath me, Christ above me,
Christ in quiet, Christ in danger,
Christ in the hearts of all that love me,
Christ in mouth of friend and stranger."

Patrick found something of Christ in everything, even in his suffering.

Patrick didn't have a faith that asked God to protect him from suffering. He went through too much in his life to hope for that. He was just looking for the presence of Christ in all things, including in suffering. Certainly Patrick could have affirmed the words of the Apostle Paul: "Suffering produces endurance, and endurance produces character, and character produces hope, and hope does not disappoint us, because God's love has been poured into our hearts through the Holy Spirit which has been given to us." (Romans 5:3-5, RSV).

Saint Patrick personified another passage from Saint Paul: the epistle lesson assigned for this Sunday. Patrick could have said this: "I want to know Christ and the power of his resurrection and the sharing of his sufferings by becoming like him in his death, if somehow I may attain the resurrection from the dead. Not that I have already obtained this or have already reached the goal; but I press on to make it my own, because Christ Jesus has made me his own...I do not consider that I have made it my own; but this one thing I do: forgetting what lies behind and straining forward to what lies ahead, I press on toward the goal for the prize of the heavenly call of God in Christ Jesus" (Philippians 3. 10-14, NRSV)

"*Go Neirigh An Bothar Libh, Slan Agus Vannacht*" ("Ga nearing an bother live, slan agus vannech.") That's my best Irish for "May the road rise to greet you, and may God bless you." May something of Saint Patrick — his faith, his courage, his ability to find Christ in all things — go with you on your life's "journey." Who knows what *we* might do with our lives if *we* had that kind of faith?

Saints Alive – Francis of Assisi: "Knight Of Christ"

Matthew 5: 1-11.

For centuries the church has celebrated "All Saints' Day" on October 31. Actually, All Saints Day was created to counteract a pagan holiday, which has sneaked back in as Halloween. But any Sunday can be an opportunity to lift up the saints of the church. I'd like us to think about Saint Francis of Assisi today. When I read the Beatitudes, I often think of him. If anyone lived these "beautiful attitudes," if anyone was "poor in spirit"' (and in reality), if anyone was "hungry and thirsty" for righteousness (and in life), if anyone was "merciful," "pure in heart"' and a "peacemaker," it was Francis. In fact, Francis is probably most people's favorite saint (with the possible exception of Saint Nicholas).

Francis was born in the Italian hill town of Assisi in 1181 or 1182.[5] His given name was Giovanni de Bernadoni — Giovanni, the son of Bernadoni. But his father, a prominent cloth merchant nicknamed his son "Francesco," "the French One," because Francis' mother was French. The nickname took.

Francis grew up the pampered, somewhat spoiled son and heir of doting, wealthy parents. His youth was spent in "wine, women, and song." Like many young men of his time, Francis aspired to be a knight. Since Francis was not born into a noble family, his only way

---

5 William Cook and Ronald Herzman, *Francis of Assisi* (Chantilly, VA: The Teaching Company Great Courses no. 615, 2000) is another well-produced and engaging series of videotaped lectures, this time on Francis's life.

to be knighted was to win honor in battle. At age twenty Francis went off to war against a neighboring town. The battle went badly and Francis was captured. He languished in prison camp for a year. During that time Francis became ill. Francis became ill and nearly died. Eventually his family was allowed to ransom him. Francis came back from war a changed man.

The party life and even inheriting the family business no longer seemed important. He began wandering the hills at night. One night, while praying in a ruined chapel, he thought he heard the crucifix speak. "Rebuild my church" is what the crucified figure said. Francis took the command literally and, with the help of some friends, brick by brick, rebuilt the broken-down church. They went on to repair other ruined chapels.

Francis, increasingly religious, made a pilgrimage to Rome. While there he joyfully exchanged his rich clothes for those of a beggar. His father, Bernadoni, was starting to lose patience with his odd, sensitive son. He wanted Francis to "get down to business" selling cloth. He finally lost his temper when Francis traded a bolt of expensive cloth for building materials to rebuild yet another church.

Bernadoni dragged Francis by the ear to the Bishop of Assisi. He expected the bishop to talk some sense into his son, maybe quote the fifth commandment, "Honor your father and mother." But Francis impulsively stripped off all his clothes in the central square of Assisi and, standing stark naked, handed them back to his father. He would no longer accept anything from him. From then on Francis would depend completely on God.

Francis resolved to follow Jesus literally. He took as his guide Jesus' words on sending off his disciples:

as you travel, take no bread, no bag, and no money, wear only one cloak and sandals (Mark 6:9). Francis, 25 years old, never again touched money — ever. He cheerfully embraced extreme poverty for the remaining twenty years of his life. It was said of Francis that he was as hungry for poverty as most other people are for gold.

After leaving his father, Francis first went to live with the lepers. He later called this the single happiest time in his life. But soon other idealistic young men were drawn to Francis and his path of joy through commitment and self-denial. A band of brothers followed him. Francis led them to Rome.

There he requested an audience with the pope and, almost miraculously, received one. The ragged young man met Pope Innocent the Third, one of the great Medieval popes. Francis requested the pope's permission to form an order of brothers — monks. They were to be begging friars. Their special mission was to preach repentance. Innocent the Third granted his permission and in 1209 the Franciscans were formed.

They were a new kind of monks. The world was their cloister. Francis and his brothers traveled constantly, preaching and begging. They had no home. They slept wherever they could, in barns, or haystacks, often out-of-doors, even in ovens. In spite of the hardships, Francis felt fulfilled. He was close to nature and close to God. During this period Francis wrote songs, prayers, and poetry, including his famous "canticle of the creatures," the first known prayer in Italian and the basis for the beloved hymn, "All Creatures Of Our God And King."

Francis, who once went off to war, gained a reputation as a peacemaker. He frequently was sought to make peace between warring towns. On one occasion when fighting threatened to break out within a town, he calmed the community by composing a song. Another time he walked all the way to the Near East with the fifth crusade. He didn't go to fight but to preach to the sultan, which he did. Fearless Francis impressed Saladin, the sultan. Saladin didn't convert to Christianity or stop the fighting, but he sent Francis back to Italy with a rich caravan of gifts, which the embarrassed Francis gave to the poor. Francis became, in his own way, a knight for Christ.

Francis was an innovative preacher. In 1223, on Christmas Eve, he created the first Christmas creche anywhere, using live animals, to make Christmas "come alive." He not only reached people, he even preached to birds. I'm not sure what the birds thought of Francis' preaching. But it's significant that Francis wanted to bring Christ to "all creatures of our God." His emphasis on the sacredness of creation inspired the Roman Catholic Church to declare Francis the patron saint of ecology.[6]

Within just a few decades Franciscans spread as far north as Norway and as far east as China. Francis also founded, "The Third Order." This was a spiritual discipline designed for lay men and women. If you joined the Third Order (as tens of thousands did, including the poet Dante) you committed yourself to a life of charity, simplicity, and non-violence. Francis led a genuine spiritual renewal in the medieval world.[7]

6   If the order of this series is followed, with one sermon on a saint per month, Francis would be preached on in April. Francis's ecological emphasis might be connected to Earth Day, April 22.

7   Philip Daileader, *The High Middle Ages* (Chantilly, VA: The Teaching Company Great Courses no. 867, 2001), Part I, Lecture 10 describes the impact of Francis and the Franciscans across Medieval Europe.

Through the Franciscans' especially their service to the poor, his work continues today.

Like Jesus, Francis lived close to God and spread joy and peace. Also like Jesus, Francis died young. He wore himself out with poverty, praying, and preaching and died when he was only 45. The last thing he dictated before dying was a verse in his "canticle of the creatures." In it he praised and embraced "Sister Death."

What might we say about Saint Francis of Assisi? What meaning might this saint's life have for us in the twenty-first century? Someone has said that Francis of Assisi is the most admired and least emulated of all the saints. Few of us would be able to – or want to — attempt the kind of life Francis lived.

But maybe remembering Francis can expand our understanding of what a really committed Christian can accomplish. We probably won't affect our entire age as he did. But certainly we can make an impact for the good on our family, our neighborhood, our church, maybe even our community. Francis' life speaks to me of the power of commitment, especially the need of standing up for the poor.

It also makes me think some of the things I often think are so important maybe really aren't so important. For twenty years, Francis had nothing: no fixed address, no savings, not even an extra blanket. He couldn't even be sure where his next meal was coming from. All he had was his relationship with God.

Was Francis unhappy or afraid? As near as I can tell, he wasn't. Quite the contrary, he seemed to radiate a kind of infectious joy. During his own life, several thousand men, knowing exactly how he lived, chose to become Franciscans with him. Thousands of women joined their sister order, the Clares.

They didn't join the Franciscans or the Clares because they were masochists. Rather they perceived Francis had discovered a way to a truly happy life. His followers were willing to pay the cost of discipleship to receive God's greater blessings: including joy even in the face of extreme poverty and suffering. Their witness challenges me to expand my horizons. If they could do — and did do — that much for Jesus, can't I do more myself? Won't I do more?

Which brings us back to where we began, back to the Beatitudes. In this passage, "Blessed" is better translated "happy." Maybe it's better to read the Beatitudes like this:

> Happy are the poor in spirit, for theirs is the kingdom of heaven.
> Happy are those who mourn, for they will be comforted.
> Happy are the meek, for they will inherit the earth.
> Happy are those who hunger and thirst for righteousness, for they will be filled.
> Happy are the merciful, for they will receive mercy.
> Happy are the pure in heart, for they will see God.
> Happy are the peacemakers, for they will be called the children of God.

The life of Saint Francis makes me believe all the above can be true.

Saints Alive – Elizabeth Seton: "Saintly Mother"

Proverbs 31 (selected verses); 1 Corinthians 13: 4-8a.

This year I'm preaching on a Roman Catholic saint a month. "Saints Alive" is what I'm calling my series. This month our Saints Alive sermon falls on Mother's Day. I looked through the list of saints to see if any were mothers. Turns out being a saint and a mother doesn't go together much — at least in the Roman Catholic Church!

Almost all the female saints — and there are hundreds — are either young women who never married, or nuns, or widows whose children were raised. One female saint was even praised for giving up her children. She didn't want anything to come between her and God! Not a great illustration for Mother's Day — at least not to me!

Then I stumbled on Saint Elizabeth Ann Seton. Elizabeth: that's my mother's name. It was my mother-in-law's, too. Good choice! Turns out Elizabeth Seaton is a great example of a saintly mother. Her story is interesting. She has a lot to teach us about mothering your own children, and being a mother-figure to others. So, here's a sermon on Elizabeth Ann Seton, who happens to be the first woman elevated to sainthood in America.

She was born in New York City in 1774, just before the Revolution. Her family was sophisticated, well-educated, and wealthy. Elizabeth's father was a physician who was the first professor of anatomy at Columbia

University, which was only twenty years old at the time. Later he was chief health officer for the City of New York. Her mother was the daughter of a prominent Episcopalian priest. Elizabeth was raised Protestant. Even at a young age she was devoted to good works.

At age twenty she married William Seaton, a wealthy merchant. Their marriage was happy, but short. William supported her charity work, as she served the needs of the city's poor. Like "the good wife" described in Proverbs 31, Elizabeth "opened her hand to the (needy)." This in addition to mothering her own five children.

Unfortunately this charming, well-bred woman, who did so much for the poor, soon faced poverty herself. Her husband lost his fortune and his health to tuberculosis. Doctors advised him to move to Italy, where the climate was warm. So the Setons sailed for Italy, where he hoped to recover. Arriving in Italy, they were quarantined for two years. William's health — and depression — got worse. Elizabeth, the good wife, tried to raise his spirits. Like Proverbs 31, she did her husband good, not harm, all the days of his life. She cared for him, and tried to cheer him. Still, William died within two years. Elizabeth was widowed, with five small children to raise alone, at age 29.

She stayed on in Italy for two more years, where she was exposed to Roman Catholicism. On returning to New York, she converted, even though there was prejudice against Catholics. Some states had anti-Catholic laws for a 150 years. Elizabeth knew becoming a Catholic would end all financial support from her husband's family. It did. They cut Elizabeth and her children off completely. That's why she's the patron saint of those who are rejected for their faith — also the patron saint of in-law troubles! (So, if your in-laws sometimes seem more like outlaws, here's a saint for you!)

More heartaches came. Two of her children, like her husband, died from tuberculosis. She's additionally the patron saint for those who lose children. She worked hard running a boarding house. As Proverbs puts it, she did not "eat the bread of idleness." Her "lamp did not go out at night," because she was up late, working.

In time, her industry and devotion caught the eye of church officials. Elizabeth was invited to start a school for poor Catholic children. It was the first-ever American parochial school. She's also the patron saint of Catholic schools! Elizabeth Seton, who never remarried, became Mother Superior of a new Roman Catholic order, the Sisters of Charity of Saint Vincent de Paul. Her elevation was approved personally by John Carroll, the first American bishop.

At the time, hers were the only non-cloistered nuns in America. That is, the only sisters who actually got out of the convent and worked among the poor. They were devoted to the needy, and built the first Catholic orphanage (making Elizabeth additionally the patron saint of orphanages!). Over time the Sisters of Charity evolved into six separate orders with thousands of nuns. They continue today.

Elizabeth Seton accomplished all this just sixteen years after becoming a Catholic — all before she died, like her husband and two children, of tuberculosis. She was only 46! Today this remarkable woman and mother has her name carved above the doors of Saint Patrick's Cathedral in New York. Seton Hall University, a Big East sports powerhouse is named for her.

So are four other colleges, 35 parishes and fifty Catholic schools. What a legacy from a woman who raised five children, converted late, was ill the last years of her life and then died young!

Throughout her life, Elizabeth "opened her mouth with wisdom." Seton is one of the most quotable saints. It was she who said, "Live simply so that others can simply live," which has become a motto of ecology. She said, "(God) is more within us than we are ourselves." She said, "Disorder in society is the result of disorder in the family." There are all surprisingly up-to-date ideas for a woman who lived mostly in the 1700's!

Turns out she was a great mother, too. Her children rose up to call her blessed, as Proverbs puts it. Her surviving daughter, Catherine, became the first nun to join another Order. She spent her career counseling prisoners and was known as "The Prison Sister." Like her mother, she was elevated to Mother Superior.

Elizabeth Seton's a wonderful example of a mother who was literally "saintly," declared a saint by the Roman Catholic Church. But I think there's something "saintly" in every good mother, who "opens her hands to the poor," "opens her mouth with wisdom," whose "children rise up and call her blessed" who, like most mothers, "does not eat the bread of idleness," whose "lamp does not go out at night."

Pope John Paul II, himself elevated to sainthood in 2014, wrote about the special qualities of mothering in one of his apostolic letters. It reads, in part:

> "Motherhood involves a special communion with the mystery of life, as it develops in the mother's womb. The mother is filled with wonder at this mystery of life, and 'understands' with unique intuition what is

happening inside her. In the light of the 'beginning', the mother accepts and loves as a person the child she is carrying in her womb. This unique contact with the new human being developing within her gives rise to an attitude toward human beings — not only toward her own child, but every human being — which profoundly marks the woman's personality."[8]

Kahlil Gibran, the Lebanese-American poet wrote this about mothers:

> "The most beautiful word on the lips of mankind is the word 'Mother,' and the most beautiful call is the call of 'My mother.' It is a word full of hope and love, a sweet and kind word coming from the depths of the heart. The mother is everything—she is our consolation in sorrow, our hope in misery, and our strength in weakness. She is the source of love, mercy, sympathy, and forgiveness."

Touching, right!? There's a couple of "warm fuzzies" for Mother's Day! But, before you get too choked up or nostalgic, here's some humor about what our "saintly mothers" taught us. Most mothers have a sense of humor, don't they? Isn't kind of necessary for survival? Here are "Things Our Mothers Taught Us:"

> Our mothers taught us religion: "You'd better pray that stain comes out of the rug."
> Our mothers taught us weather: "Your room looks like a tornado went through."
> Our mothers taught us anticipation: "Just wait until your father gets home!"
> Our mothers taught us stamina: "You'll sit there until all your spinach is gone."
> Our mothers taught us about our roots:" Close that door. Do you think you were born in a barn?"

---

8   John Paul II, *Mulieris Dignitatem*, no. 18 (1988).

Our mothers taught us logic: "Because I said so, that's why!"[9]

But most of all, saintly mothers teach us love. Love that is "patient and kind, not jealous or boastful or arrogant or rude; Love that did not insist on always getting its own way...love that bears all things, believes all things, hopes all things and endures all things. Love that never ends" (1 Cor. 13.4-8, RSV, adapted).

Love is the most precious gift from a saintly mother. Maybe the biggest joy and challenge is being "saintly" within the joys and challenges of everyday family living; for, as Pope John Paul II put it, "the home is the domestic church." Elizabeth Seaton did this wonderfully. So she, for me, becomes another patron saint: the patron saint of "saintly" mothers.

---

[9] Adapted from http://www.scrapbook.com, Author Unknown

Saints Alive – Thomas Aquinas: "The Angelic Doctor"

Ephesians 5:15-20

This past week I conducted an informal survey. I asked a random sample of half a dozen people, "How would you like to hear a sermon on Saint Thomas Aquinas?" No one said, "Yes, please," not even to be polite! Several individuals indicated they weren't quite sure who Thomas Aquinas was, although they'd heard of him. Others knew exactly who he was — and that was the problem.

One woman, on hearing his name, had an almost violent reaction: probably a bad flashback memory from freshman philosophy class. Saint Thomas Aquinas lived just a little after Saint Francis of Assisi (who, after Saint Nicholas and maybe Saint Patrick, is almost everyone's favorite saint). However, according to my brief, unscientific survey, Thomas Aquinas didn't appear to be *anyone's* favorite saint. Hopefully, by the end of this sermon, some attitudes toward Thomas might change.

By the way, college students, heading off to or returning to college, might especially want to pay attention today. Because Saint Thomas will come up in your schooling. You'll hear about him in ethics, philosophy, medieval history, political science, as well as in religion. So, you might consider this an enhancement to your education.

Thomas Aquinas was born around 1225 CE in his family's castle in southern Italy.[10] He was the last of eleven children. Thomas' father was the Count of Aquino, and related to royalty as well. His cousin was Frederick the Second, called "The Wonder of the World," who was the Holy Roman Emperor. Another relative was the king of Sicily, a third the king of France. Thomas Aquinas was "to the manor born."

At age five, his parents sent him to the nearby Benedictine monastery of Monte Cassino, site of the famous and bloody World War II battle. Younger sons of noblemen often were sent into religious life, whether they happened to be pious or not. Since the oldest son would inherit the property and title, there was little left for younger sons to do. Monastic life was considered honorable. Perhaps his family hoped Thomas would become abbot of that wealthy monastery, like his cousin.

Thomas apparently did have a natural inclination toward religion. He was a large, solemn, serious child, who rarely spoke. So he shocked his teachers with what was said to be his first question on arriving at the monastery. Out of the blue he asked them, "What is God?" Thomas received his primary education at the Benedictine school at Monte Cassino. When he was fourteen he was sent to the newly founded University of Naples. At age nineteen he was sent from Naples to the University of Paris, at that time the greatest medieval university. He also made a decision that precipitated a family crisis. Thomas joined the "upstart" Dominican Order, also called the "Black Friars," for their

---

10 Jeremy Adams, *Thomas Aquinas: The Angelic Doctor* (Chantilly, VA: The Teaching Company Great Courses DVD no. 614, 2000). This well-produced and engaging series of videotaped lecture provides a first-rate overview of Thomas's life and thought.

black cassocks. They were also known as the Order of Preachers (O. P. for short).

The Dominicans were mendicant friars. Like the followers of Saint Francis of Assisi, the Franciscans, they were expected to live in poverty, traveling around, and preaching the word. Thomas' family was scandalized. It was one thing for him to become a monk, maybe eventually the abbot of a wealthy, well-known abbey. But becoming an impoverished, traveling preacher looked like religious fanaticism. It was if he had joined a cult. Becoming a Black Friar made Thomas a "black sheep" in his family.

His brother Rinaldo had him kidnapped and brought back to the family castle for "deprogramming." Thomas was kept in the castle, virtually a prisoner, for a year. The family tried every means possible to get him to change his mind. Legend has it his brothers even hired an attractive, lady of the night to visit Thomas in his cell to tempt him to break his vow of chastity. Thomas wasn't interested. Instead, on seeing her he rushed to the fireplace, picked out a burning log and chased the terrified woman away. Then in righteous indignation he burned the sign of the cross into his door.

Eventually his family relented and released him. Thomas moved to the Dominican house in Paris. He earned a master of arts. Then his superiors sent him to Cologne, Germany to study with Albertus Magnus, Albert the Great, the premier philosopher/theologian of his time. Thomas was a brilliant student. But his brilliance wasn't always acknowledged. Part of the problem was his appearance. He was a tall, heavy man with an enormous head. G. K. Chesterton, the British writer and wit (who himself stood six feet, two inches tall, and weighed about three hundred pounds) called Thomas Aquinas "a huge bull of a man, fat, slow, and quiet." Thomas was big, although the stories they had to cut a circle in the table before he could sit at it, due to his enormous girth, probably aren't true.

Thomas undoubtedly was aware he was physically unattractive. In a lecture on Thomas, Professor Jeremy Adams of Southern Methodist University notes Thomas once wrote that a person who presents "an ugly appearance" cannot be "wholly happy," since he is aware "he is made contemptible and despicable in the eyes of others" (translation by Vernon J. Bourke). Professor Adams wonders if Thomas was thinking of himself when he wrote those words.[11] His fellow students labeled Thomas, "the dumb ox, "with "dumb" meaning not "stupid" but "silent." His teacher, Albert the Great, however, set them straight. He predicted this dumb ox's bellows would "fill the world." And they did.

Thomas returned to the University of Paris to complete his education. He received the equivalent of the Ph.D. and began to teach. But his very presence on the faculty created controversy. The secular professors resented the presence of teachers in religious orders, like Thomas, who owed their allegiance to superiors outside the university. It didn't help that Thomas had been given a special dispensation to receive his degree without completing all the requirements. The king of France and the pope had to intervene on behalf of Thomas. It was the first of many academic controversies that would mark his career.

Teaching in the medieval university was hard work — and few worked harder than Thomas. Lectures were held five days a week. They began at six in

11 Ibid, Lecture 12.

the morning and continued, with a brief break, until noon. There often were additional lectures after lunch. Thomas also engaged in numerous, voluntary debates at night. He still found time to preach in local churches, and to author sixty titles. Later in his career, when his responsibilities multiplied, Thomas would dictate to four secretaries at once, each seated in a corner of the room' to keep up with his correspondence. He was a gifted teacher, preacher, and writer, whose goal was always to try to make things clear.

His most famous work was his *Summa Theologica*, or "summary of theology." It consisted of more than ten thousand objections and replies to critical questions about God and the world, presented in something like a dialogue form. Tomas considered issues like the existence of God, the nature of humankind, sin, salvation, ethics, marriage, and the family, politics, and aesthetics. His arguments are logical, tightly constructed, elaborate, and in their own way, beautiful. Church historian Martin Marty has compared them to the impressive, soaring, complicated Gothic cathedrals that were being constructed during Thomas' lifetime.

Among his most famous contributions were his "Five Proofs of the Existence of God." Few find these proofs of God's existence completely convincing today. But Thomas Aquinas gets credit for trying.

Another of Thomas' contributions was helping reintroduce Greek philosophy to medieval Christians: particularly the thought of Aristotle. Around Thomas' time the wisdom of classical Greece was slowly reappearing, often through Arabic translations. Merging pagan thought with Christianity, sometimes with reference to Muslim thinkers, was controversial. But Thomas courageously tried to enlarge the thinking of his day.

Interestingly, this highly rational thinker was also something of a mystic. Thomas is credited with writing hymns and prayers still in use in the Roman Catholic Church. In 1264 he entered and won a competition to write the *Office*, prayers for a new feast day, Corpus Christi, the Body of Christ, celebrating the Eucharist. Thomas lifted up the saving grace of Christ's presence in the Sacrament, with words that have become part of the Mass:

> "O saving host, O bread of life
> Thou goal of rest from pain and strife,
> Embattled are we, poor and weak,
> Grant us the health and strength we seek."

Ironically, the supremely logical and highly rational Thomas had an experience toward the end of his life that seemed to undermine logic and rationality. On December 6, 1272, while celebrating mass on the Feast of Saint Nicolas, Thomas apparently had a vision or revelation. He saw, perhaps in a flash, that everything he had written up to that point was nothing but "straw." Thomas never wrote another word after that day. He left his *Summa Theologica*, summary of theology, incomplete.

His death came within fifteen months. Thomas was summoned by the pope to help lead a church council in Lyons, France. Along the way he stopped to visit his niece at her castle. At supper he dined on eels, which possibly had gone bad. Thomas grew deathly ill. His condition may have been worsened by the bump on the head he had received that day while riding. Or, as some have speculated, Thomas Aquinas may have been poisoned. He was, after all, a member of one Europe's most powerful families and did have important political connections. In any case, he died within a short time at a nearby abbey. In 1323, less than fifty years after his death, Thomas was canonized. He came to be called "the Angelic Doctor," and was named patron saint of colleges and universities.

That's an all-too-quick sketch of the life of Saint Thomas Aquinas. In what ways can we say this saint is alive today? To me, Thomas lives on in his example of Christian commitment. Here was a man born into power and wealth that willingly gave it up. Material wealth did not tempt him. Once Thomas, standing on a hill overlooking Paris, said he would rather have a Bible commentary on Matthew than all the wealth in the city. He meant it. From his early commitment to the "radical" Dominicans, to his embrace of chastity in the face of temptation (remember the courtesan in the castle) to his life of hard work and poverty, Thomas was consistent in his commitment. To me he's a good example of taking the "hard, narrow gate." Though the way is hard, it leads to blessing (Matthew 4:14).

Secondly, Thomas reminds us that being a committed Christian shouldn't mean turning off your mind. Some say he was the greatest thinker between 500 and 1,500 CE, a period of a thousand years. Aquinas understood that reason, logic, and hard thinking must be put in the service of God. He didn't shy away from confronting the intellectual challenges of his time. In his day, that meant merging Christianity with the best of Greek thinking. Thomas loved the Lord with all his heart and with all his soul and with all his mind (Matthew 22:37-39). So must we. There's plenty of call, and room, for learning, growing, thinking hard and facing intellectual challenge in the Christian life. Like Thomas, we are called to give God the best of our minds.

Thirdly and finally, Thomas seems also to have fulfilled the second half of the Great Commandment. He not only loved God, he loved his neighbor as he loved himself. This huge man, so often made fun of by others, so often embroiled in controversies, seems not to have born anyone any ill will. In his thousands of pages of writing, Thomas never attacked anyone. It was said of him, "His soul was at once humble and sweet."

Saint Thomas Aquinas said, "To love anyone is nothing more that to wish that person good." Thomas' words and example point us back to the wonder and mystery of agape love. God has given us that kind of love, love that wishes and wills our good. We are called to love one another, as God has loved us (John 13.32). That was Jesus' new commandment. Thomas Aquinas tried to live it out. That sounds like a pretty good summary of theology to me.

Saints Alive – Kateri Tekakwitha: "Lily of the Mohawks"

Psalm 103: 1-8; Matthew 5: 1-11.

The first dozen years of my ministry were spent in upstate New York. Often, on my day off, my wife and I took road trips through that lovely landscape. One spot we visited was The National Shrine of the North American Martyrs near Albany.

This huge site, with a circular coliseum seating 6,000, is dedicated to three martyrs from the 1640's: a lay missionary, a Jesuit brother and a Jesuit priest. They were killed there by the Native Americans they had come to serve. It's a spectacular setting — 600 acres on a hillside overlooking the Mohawk River.

Also there is a chapel for the saint we consider this morning, Kateri Tekakwitha. Kateri was her Christian name, given at baptism. It's a derivative of Catherine. Tekakwitha was her Native American name. She's been called "The Lily of the Mohawk," "The New Star of the New World" and "The Prairie Flower." It's her story I'll to reflect on today, to bring this saint "alive."

She was born in 1656 near the shrine, the daughter of a Mohawk chief. Her mother was from another tribe, and a Christian. This was in a time when Native American believers were few and far between.

Both her parents died when Kateri was four, along with her younger brother, in a smallpox epidemic. The disease left her face badly scarred and her eyes weakened for life. One translation I've read for her Native American name, "Tekakwitha," is "The One Who

Walks Groping for Her Way." So Kateri lost her parents and her health when she was very young. Still, it's likely her mother's faith affected her profoundly. One commentator writes, "What three- or four-year-old is not aware of what her mother is doing, in this case kneeling and praying to the Great Spirit as taught her by the Black Robes (the Jesuits)?"[12]

So a first lesson we get from Kateri is the importance of a parent's faith. We never know how we might shape the spirituality of the children around us — and they're watching all the time. When they study us, do they see us living our faith?

The orphaned Kateri was adopted by an uncle, another chief. Unfortunately her uncle was hostile to Christianity. Her mother had given Kateri a rosary. Her uncle took it away. Nevertheless, she tried to live a Christian life, doing her work faithfully as an act of service, and especially tending to the needs of the sick and weak.

A priest who knew Kateri wrote, "(She) could not suffer the broad daylight on account of the weakness of her eyes. But, although she was infirm, she always was the first to be at work."[13] Kateri becomes a good example of doing our work as a gift to God. As Bernard of Clairvaux, that great reformer of monasticism, put it, "Those who labor as they pray lift their hearts to God with their hands"(adapted). Work can be a form of worship. It was for Kateri. Is it for you?

Given her privileged status, as daughter of a chief, Kateri received many marriage proposals. She refused them. She was not interested in marriage and raising a

---

12 Norm Leveillee, http:www.kateritekakwitha.org
13 Father Edward Sherman, *Tekakwitha: Holy Native, Mohawk Virgin, 1656-1680* (Grand Forks, ND: Fine Print of Grand Forks, Inc., 2007), pp. 38,31.

family, which was expected of Native American native maidens. Instead she was drawn her mother's faith. When she was twenty, a Jesuit missionary came to her village and established a chapel. Her uncle disliked the "Black Robe" and distrusted this foreign religion. But he allowed Kateri to receive instruction for baptism.

The young woman studied hard, seeking to be worthy of this blessing. The priest wrote of her, "She had learned her prayers with a quickness and eagerness that was truly marvelous.."[14] Kateri is a good example for us of taking our faith seriously, not taking it for granted. Growth in faith requires study and effort, doesn't it? Kateri was baptized, with two others, on Easter Day.

After her baptism, she tried to live her faith even more intently, but was rejected by many. Her unwillingness to marry, and attempts to keep the fourth commandment, "Remember the sabbath day, and keep it holy" (Exodus 20:8, NRSV) by not working Sundays, drew taunts. She was stoned, and received death threats. Kateri was reviled and persecuted for righteousness sake, just like the Beatitudes (see Matthew 5:10-11). But even in persecution, she felt blessed. Her perseverance teaches us the promises of the Beatitudes are true.

After over a year, when the opportunity arose, she chose to move to a Christian village in Canada. Kateri understood the wisdom of surrounding herself with other believers. So should we. Our faith is like a glowing coal. Take a burning coal away from the fire, and it quickly goes out. Surround it with other glowing coals, and it burns even brighter.

14   Ibid., p. 44

We need each other, to keep our faith burning brightly. That's why going to worship every week is important, so we can warm each other up. Kateri walked more than two hundred miles to find a village where she could live with other Christians.

The remaining three years of her life were spent in Canada. There she wholeheartedly invested herself in Christian living. Much of her time was spent in prayer, at the altar of an unheated church, even in the dead of winter. A priest wrote, "Often seeing (Kateri) benumbed with cold, I have sent her to the cabin to warm herself. She obeyed immediately, but the moment after, returned to the church, and continued there in long communion with Jesus Christ."[15]

A highlight of her life was receiving first communion, around age twenty. This she did with "all imaginable joy." Just as surprising, every succeeding time she received the sacrament, she showed the same excitement. Her enthusiasm never waned. Kateri's example was such that others tried to sit next to her in church, to catch some of the warmth and glow that shone from her.

In this she reminds me of Thomas Merton, that great writer, Trappist monk and mystic of the twentieth century. Merton wrote this about receiving the sacrament for the first time, in his case, as an adult:

> "Heaven was entirely mine...Christ, hidden in the small host, was giving himself for me and to me, and with himself the entire Godhead and Trinity...Christ was born in me, his new Bethlehem, and sacrificed in me, his new Calvary, and risen in me...(God) called out to me from his own immense depths."[16]

---

15 Ibid., p. 44.

16 Thomas Merton, *The Seven Story Mountain* (Garden City, NY: Image Books, 1970), pp. 273-274.

I wonder: do we receive Communion with the same enthusiasm as Kateri, or Thomas Merton? How would our faith change if we took this great blessing and mystery more seriously?

Kateri's faith soon began to develop in another way. I mentioned earlier she wasn't interested in marrying. She began to believe she was called to celibacy. As a perpetual virgin, she could devote her full attention to worshiping and serving God. She would, in a sense, be "married" — married to Christ.

A priest explained her commitment to Christ like this: "Some...want their body and soul to be kept special for Christ. Although different from the love that married people so rightly and holily may share, the love that a consecrated virgin shares with Christ can be equally warm and deep, and perhaps even more profound. (Kateri) for this reason would not marry; she reserved her spousal love for Christ alone."[17]

Kateri sought to live for Christ alone. She not only accepted chastity, but poverty and obedience. She knew that, in remaining unmarried, she would deny herself the material comforts a husband would provide. Yet she said:

> "I am not my own; I have given myself to Jesus. He must be my only love. The state of helpless poverty that may befall me if I do not marry does not frighten me. All I need is a little food and a few pieces of clothing. With the work of my hands I shall always earn what is necessary and what is left over I'll give to my relatives and to the poor. If I should become sick and unable to work, then I shall be like the Lord on the cross. He will have mercy on me and help me, I am sure."[18]

---

17 Sherman, p. 68.
18 faithofthefatherssaintquote.blogspot.com

In time, due to ill health and hard work, plus self-imposed sufferings, like sleeping on thorns, in imitation of Jesus, who wore a crown of thorns, Kateri wore herself out. She died at age 24. According to witnesses, her last words were "Jesus, I love you" whispered to her divine lover. She died peacefully, as if entering into a light sleep.

Kateri's whole life was something of a miracle. A miracle surrounded her death. When you see pictures of her, she almost always looks beautiful. In reality, her face was badly pock-marked, from the smallpox that afflicted her as a child. But, at her death, those scars disappeared. Kateri went to heaven unmarked. This miracle was witnessed and attested to by two priests, and others who were with her. It echoes Psalm 103, the psalm for today, where David promises God "heals all your diseases."(v. 3b, NRSV). Kateri's remains are buried in a chapel in Canada, which has become a place of pilgrimage.

Her short life was filled with loss, illness, rejection, hard work, voluntary suffering, poverty, chastity, and obedience. Was it wasted? No! For one thing her example is alive in Kateri circles. These are prayer and support groups, popular among Native Americans, that encourage daily devotions, deeds of loving kindness and education about Native American issues. You can find them on nearly every reservation, and in cities in North America where there are large Native American populations. In a sense, she lives on in them.

Plus Kateri challenges us to stretch beyond mere pleasure seeking. Too often our attentions are directed to what's easiest and most pleasurable for us. Too many Americans, including Christians, live by the motto "If it feels good, you should."

Kateri offers a different approach. Her life was blessed, even in the face of grief, suffering, loss, and persecution — not because it was easy, but because she lived it in close connection to Christ. The Roman Catholic Bishop of Albany writes:

> "In this day and age, when the pleasure-principle so dominates our society, and when people expend all kinds of time, effort, and energy to remove the cross from Christianity and to escape the sometimes harsh realities and responsibilities of mature Christian living, Kateri Tekakwitha stands as an heroic example of how to integrate the mystery of the Cross with the mystery of the resurrection in a way that gives honor and glory to God and that ensures loving service to (God's) people."[19]

Kateri proved the poor in spirit, those who mourn, the meek, the hungry and thirsty for righteousness, the merciful, the pure in heart, the peacemakers, and those persecuted and reviled for righteousness sake, can be blessed, happy. Because a relationship with Jesus is worth it.

No cross, no crown.

That makes her the Lily of the Mohawks, a symbol of resurrection, and a good example Christian living for you and me. She was rightly honored in 2012 as the first Native American saint.

---

19 The Most Reverend Howard J. Hubbard, quoted at http://conservation.catholic.org, website of the Saint Kateri Tekakwitha Conservation Center, Inc.

Saints Alive – Father Damien: "Contagious Faith"

Luke 17:1-11.

In the gospel lesson I read, ten lepers approach Jesus near a village. Standing apart, as the law demanded, they beg him to "have mercy" and heal them from their disease. Exactly what that disease was isn't completely clear. Sometimes what the Bible labels leprosy isn't Hansen's Disease, that horrifying, progressive, contagious condition that attacks nerve endings and destroys skin and limbs. What scripture labels leprosy also could be psoriasis or eczema — unpleasant, but less serious ailments.

Still, there were lepers in Jesus' day. Records of this disease go back four thousand years. Plus even if all ten men weren't *actual* lepers, they were treated *like* lepers, separated from their families, unwelcome in the village, they had to announce their presence by shouting "unclean, unclean."

Lepers were viewed as terrible sinners. It was believed God sent this ugly disease as a punishment. Miserable disease must equal miserable sinner, right? So we understand why these ten men longed to be healed. They wanted their health, lives, livelihood, families, and reputations back: not surprising.

What's surprising, astonishing, is the saint we consider today. Father Damien was a Belgian priest who voluntarily lived for sixteen years where he was likely to *become* a leper. Jesus said, "Greater love has no man than this, that a man lay down his life for his friends" (John 15:13, RSV). Father Damien showed that "greater love." He's an example of contagious faith.

There was nothing remarkable about Damien's early life. He was born Jozef DeVeuster in 1840 in Belgium. His father was a corn merchant. Jozef was expected to take over the business. But at age eighteen he received a call to ministry, like his older brother. Jozef wasn't a great student. Some didn't think he had the makings of a priest. But his brother tutored him in Latin, the language of the mass. His grasp was sufficiently good to get him into seminary. Jozef was a hard-working, serious young man, also physically powerful. But he was also strong in faith. He prayed daily to Saint Francis Xavier, patron saint of missionaries, to be sent to a mission.

When he was 24, he got his chance. His older brother had been assigned to Hawaii, but was ill. Jozef took his place. He sailed for 148 days straight, from a port in Germany to Hawaii. On arriving, he was ordained, and took the name Damien, after an ancient physician-saint who was martyred for Christ.

Next he learned Hawaiian, a difficult language. Then Damien spent seven years doing the extraordinary ordinary work of a missionary priest. His "parish" was a thousand square miles. There were few roads. He often traveled by mule. Some mountains too steep even for a mule. He climbed them on foot. Other islands could only be reached by canoe over treacherous waters. It took six weeks for Damien to make his rounds, saying mass and hearing confessions. Then he started over again. Most of the time, he was alone. Priests were too scarce to assign two to a parish.

Meanwhile Hawaii was in crisis. Foreign traders and sailors brought leprosy to the islands. The government's response was to quarantine every leper they could find into isolated colonies, to prevent its spread. On Molokai was a colony of eight hundred lepers. Many were Roman Catholic. They begged the bishop for a priest. He acknowledged their need, but knew the risks. He would not order any priest to such a place.

Four priests volunteered. They each were to spend several weeks or a month alone at the colony, then rotate out, to reduce their exposure. Damien was first to go. He was inspired, in part, by stories of Jesus healing lepers. Conditions in the colony were terrible. Law and order were gone. Fighting, drunkenness, theft, and rape were rampant. Little good food was provided. Lepers scavenged like animals for scraps. They lived in caves or shacks. Death was constant. Bodies were dumped in shallow pits, where they often were eaten by wild dogs or pigs. The sights and smells were unbearable.

In total chaos, where do you start creating order? Damien began by restoring dignity to the dying. Like his physician-saint namesake, he dressed their open sores. He built coffins and dug graves himself, fenced in a cemetery, and conducted funeral masses. Largely alone, he built a church. Here his remarkable strength and carpenter skills paid off. Gavin Davis, in his excellent biography, *Holy Man: Father Damien of Molokai*, labeled the hearty priest "God's athlete."[20]

After a short stay, seeing progress, Damien begged his bishop to stay. The request was granted. Damien committed himself completely to the lepers. He made this fateful decision around Easter, the date of Christ's

---

20 Gavan Davis, *Holy Man: Father Damien of Molokai* (Honolulu, HI: University of Hawaii Press, 1984), p. 53.

death and resurrection. He was 33 years old, the age of Jesus at his death. It would result in what one writer called Father Damien's "peculiar Golgotha."[21] For the remaining sixteen years of his life, Damien lived with the lepers. He wrote his priest brother, "I make myself a leper with the lepers to gain all to Jesus Christ."

Over the years Damien transformed the colony. He guided the residents in building decent houses. Together they created farms, schools, orphanages, a clinic, a harbor and even children's choirs and marching bands. Damien also was adept at using publicity to demand better conditions for the lepers. This made him few friends among the authorities, who labeled him "obstinate" and "headstrong." A critic called him a "course, dirty man." Even his religious superior accused him of dipping his pen in acid, when he insisted on getting better medicines and supplies.

Nevertheless, he was effective. A visitor to the colony wrote, "I had gone to Molokai expecting to find it scarcely less dreadful than hell itself, and the cheerful people, the lovely landscapes, and comparatively painless life were all surprises. These poor people seemed singularly happy." Remarkable change, right?

Of course, Damien constantly was exposed to a deadly disease. Leprosy is not as contagious as you might think, but it is contagious. After living eleven years in daily contact with lepers, one day Father Damien noticed something. Preparing to bathe, he stepped into hot water, but felt nothing, even while his skin blistered. He'd lost feeling in his foot. He knew the signs well. Father Damien had become a leper. From the start, when he preached he spoke to his parishioners as "we lepers." He knew eventually his words would come truc. They did.

21   Ibid., p. 124.

Damien lived another four and one-half years, as his body rotted. Knowing he was dying, he threw himself more feverishly into his work. Damien said, "I would not be cured if the price of the cure was that I must leave the island and give up my work... I am perfectly resigned to my lot. Do not feel sorry for me."

His faith was contagious. Others joined him. Toward the end of his life helpers arrived: another priest, a former Civil War officer who was a recovering alcoholic, a male nurse, and several nuns. They reported Damien working into the final stages of his illness, one arm in a sling, a foot in bandages, and a leg dragging behind him. He died of leprosy after a brief confinement, and was buried on one of the cemeteries he'd created. He was 49.

Father Damien was gone. But his work continued. Others, like Mother Superior Marianne Cope, and the sisters who came with her, carried it on. She was willing to suffer, as Damien did. Mother Marianne wrote, "...I am hungry for the work and I wish with all my heart to be one of the chosen ones, whose privilege it will be, to sacrifice themselves for the salvation of the souls of the poor islanders....I am not afraid of any disease, hence it would be my greatest delight even to minister to the abandoned 'lepers.'" But, while she lived there for thirty years, constantly in contact with leprosy, she never caught it. The Roman Catholic Church considers this a miracle, and has put Mother Marianne on the path to sainthood.

Damien's example of selfless love inspired others worldwide. The late Mother Teresa studied him closely. So did Mahatma Gandhi, who wrote there are "very few heroes who can compare with Father Damien..."

Maybe the greatest tribute is from lepers themselves. With modern medicines, leprosy isn't contagious. But a hundred or so lepers still live in the Molokai colony. They're free to leave.

As one commentator put it, "By the time they repealed the (quarantine) law...most of the people in the community had been there for thirty, forty, or fifty years. It was the only home they had...They had formed a magnificent sort of loving community that, over the years, had also turned into one of the last unspoiled places in Hawaii." From a hellhole to a heaven, thanks, in large part, to the courageous, contagious faith of a Belgian priest.

In what way is this saint "alive" today? Damien reminds us no one is too unlovely for God — and by extension beyond our Christian concern. He's the patron saint of lepers, but also the HIV positive, AIDS sufferers, and outcasts.

We hope God, and others, will love us when we are unlovely, scarred by stupidity or sin. So also we are to extend agape love to all. In Christ's name, we are to offer what one denomination, the United Church of Christ (UCC) calls "an extravagant welcome." As the UCC puts it, "No matter who you are, or where you are on life's journey, you are welcome here." I hope that's true of all Christ's churches.

Father Damien also reminds following Christ sometimes means suffering. Jesus suffered. We inevitably will, too. A letter attributed to Saint Paul, Second Timothy, puts it like this: "Remember Jesus Christ, raised from the dead...that is my gospel, for which I suffer... even to the point of being chained like a criminal." "But," Paul continues, "the word of God is not chained (or confined by any condition or disease). Therefore I endure everything for the sake of the elect... The saying is sure: If we have died with (Christ), we will also live with him; if we endure, we will also reign with him..." (2.8-12a, NRSV).

Like Saint Paul, Saint Damien suffered hardship, was an outcast, endured much, died to self, and lived for Christ and others. Now he reigns forever with Christ in heaven. He discovered, as II Timothy puts it, Christ "remains faithful — for he cannot deny himself' (2:13, NRSV).

God does not abandon us in our suffering. Rather God can use even suffering for a purpose. No situation, no matter how terrible, is beyond God's redemption. We see that clearly in Christ on the cross, So Damien becomes a Christ figure, reminding us of all the unjustified suffering Jesus endured, for you and me.

Finally, Damien reminds us that miracles do happen. He never cured a leper, like Jesus did. But his love changed the lives for the better of thousands of lepers who came though that colony — and his contagious faith inspired the world. Sometimes love and self-sacrifice is miraculous in itself. Christian love changes things. That's good news!

Saints Alive – Katharine Drexel: "Poor Little Rich Girl"

Matthew 25:31-46.

Sixty years ago, in 1955, an elderly woman died in a small, second-floor room in a Philadelphia suburb. She was 96. For almost twenty years she'd been confined to that room, since her first heart attack, at age 77. She'd lived most of her life in poverty. She stretched a pair of shoes so they lasted ten years. She only ate the simplest foods. She used pencils down to the stub. At death she owned some clothing, rosary beads, and odd scraps of paper and notebooks, filled with her thoughts and prayers.

Her most prized possession *had been* a picture of the pope. She'd held it in her hands for hours as she prayed. But she'd given that to a friend who seemed to be down, hoping to lift his spirits. At death this woman had almost nothing to her name.

But what a name it was: Katharine Drexel! She was born, with not a silver spoon but a gold spoon in her mouth. Her father was one of the wealthiest and most prominent men in the world, a founding partner of Drexel, Morgan, and Company. Morgan was J. P Morgan of J. P. Morgan Chase, the world's sixth-largest bank. Katharine's father was a partner with J. P. Morgan! The Drexels lived in mansions and traveled in their own private railroad cars. Katharine was a highly educated, sophisticated, widely traveled debutant. Still, she gave it up for a life of poverty. She also gave her entire fortune away — some one hundred sixty million dollars in today's money.

If you had a hundred sixty million dollars, don't you think you might be tempted to "reverse tithe," — give most of it away, but keep 10% back for yourself, and feel you'd done enough? You'd be really generous, and still have sixteen million dollars!

Katharine reminds me of Richie Rich, from the comic books of my youth. Remember Richie Rich, the "poor little rich boy?" She was a "poor little rich girl." She was born rich, but died poor, with nothing. Or did she? Katharine Drexel is the saint we consider today.

She was born in Philadelphia in 1858, the middle of three sisters. Her mother died when Katharine was five weeks old. Two years later her father remarried. Both father and stepmother were devout Roman Catholics. They shaped Katharine into the person she would be.

Three afternoons a week her mother opened their mansion to the poor. With the help of advisers, she personally considered hundreds of requests from the needy every year. Worthy individuals received cash for medicine or rent on the spot. Meals and clothing also were provided right there at the mansion. Mrs. Drexel personally gave away several hundred thousand dollars a year (in today's money), while meeting the poor face-to-face.

Newspapers wrote not of the gala parties she threw but about her faithful service to "the poor, the sick, the unemployed (and) the dying." They noted, "The families she...aided can be numbered in the hundreds" and "few women ever secured so many jobs" for the unemployed. Meanwhile, Katharine's father was on the board of directors for many Philadelphia charities.

Katharine learned from their example to care about and for the less fortunate. Plus they set an example of daily prayer. When her stepmother designed their mansion, she had a chapel built in. They used it daily for family devotions.

Busy as he was, her father retired to the chapel to pray, alone, for a half an hour a day. Unfortunately, both her father and stepmother died when Katharine was in her twenties. She nursed her stepmother personally, while she died from a painful cancer. These losses made Katharine ponder the meaning of life.

Early on she'd developed a special concern for Native Americans. She'd seen their poverty on reservations during a trip to Montana. This prompted financial support for Indian missions. When she was in her late twenties, on a trip to Europe, Katharine had an audience with the pope. She dropped to her knees and pleaded he send more missionaries to Native Americans.

To her astonishment, his holiness asked, "Why not, my child, become a missionary yourself?" This shocked her. The very thought made her physically ill. But the pope's question opened Katharine's mind to new possibilities. Eventually it led her to a new direction. She resolved to turn her back on wealth and privilege, and join a religious order. Her first choice was for the peaceful life of a cloistered nun. She'd devote herself to prayer, in imitation of her pious parents.

But her spiritual director, a bishop, helped refine her calling. He would not allow her to enter the convent until she was thirty. Then he convinced Katharine to avoid a quiet, cloistered life for a life of prayer plus hands-on service, like that of her stepmother. He talked her into founding a new order serving the poorest of the poor. She was to underwrite it with her personal fortune.

Katharine became mother superior of an order devoted to Native Americans and African Americans. She longed to be rid of her wealth all at once, to be freed from the responsibility of managing that much money. But her spiritual director advised her to hold onto her fortune. She was to be a good steward, and invest it in missions. Katharine lived in extreme poverty herself, without most material pleasures, while slowly giving away one hundred sixty million dollars. It was a complete reversal of fortune, and one of the ironies of her life.

Most of her giving was anonymous. Usually she provided funds to start up a mission — just enough to get it going. Then other wealthy Roman Catholics were approached to keep the work funded. That way the project wouldn't dependent only on her. Her initial seed money brought forth a harvest of other people's giving.

By 1955, when Katharine died, her order numbered over five hundred nuns. They ran some 25 schools for African Americans in thirteen states, and fifty Indian missions across the West. The order also founded Xavier University in New Orleans. Today it's the only predominately black Roman Catholic university in America. By the time she died, Katharine's money was all gone.

Hers was a lifetime of successful work, undertaken in the face of opposition. Segregationists burned down one of her schools. Another time she was threatened by the klan when she built an orphanage for African Americans in Louisiana. Klansmen threatened to murder Katharine, her nuns, and the children, and burn the school down around them. But before they could attack, a few days later, the local klan headquarters was struck by lightning and completely destroyed! Another irony, and lesson — don't mess with Mother Katharine!

In Pennsylvania, at the mother house, a stick of dynamite was discovered just before the archbishop was to visit and rededicate the structure. The ceremony went on, but under police guard. So much for the quiet life of contemplation Katharine desired!

Katharine had her first heart attack at 77. Under doctor's orders, she was confined to that small, upstairs room, which she rarely left, for almost twenty years. Her life, which could have been so comfortable, was a triumph of courage in the face of adversity. But she didn't feel sorry for herself. She wrote, "The patient and humble endurance of the cross — whatever nature it may be — is the highest work we have to do."

Katharine fed the hungry, gave drink to the thirsty, clothed the naked, cared for the sick and visited the imprisoned. That's Matthew 5:31-40. Like Jesus, she "emptied" herself, "taking the form of a servant." That's Philippians 2:7. Like Christ, though she was rich, she became poor, so that out of her poverty others could be enriched. That's 2 Corinthians 8:9.

She not only served "the least and last." She also worked for racial justice. She questioned practices of the Bureau of Indian Affairs, and our nation's treatment of Native Americans. She funded NAACP investigations into the exploitation of black workers. She launched a letter-writing campaign to President Franklin Delano Roosevelt, encouraging him to address these injustices.

She was a friend and advocate to the least among us.

What lessons can we take from Katharine's life? In what sense is this saint "alive" today? One thing she reminds me of is stewardship. She could have spent her fortune on mansions, country estates, private planes, yachts, and limousines. She could have spent her time planning parties, attending the opera or on round-the-world cruises. Instead she gave it all up. How did Katharine measure her treasure? She measured it in Native American and African American children clothed and fed, in injustice and prejudice fought, and in young black women and men receiving a quality education.

Someday, as our scripture lesson suggests, we each will stand in judgment before God. That's scary. But it's in the Bible. I've got to wonder how God will measure our treasure and weigh our lives. I wonder if God, the ultimate owner of everything will be much impressed by the things that often impress us: having a nice car, or a big home, or lots of money in the bank.

Scripture says God has a different standard and that Katharine Drexel, who had all those things, but gave them up, was truly rich. That makes me wonder where I might need to change my values and my lifestyle to get them more in line with God's.

Jesus says, "Do not store up for yourselves treasures on earth, where moth and rust consume and thieves break in and steal but store up for yourselves treasures in heaven, where neither moth nor rust consumes and where thieves do not break in and steal. For where your treasure is, there will your heart be also." (Matthew 6:19-21, NRSV). Katharine Drexel lived Jesus' command. She invested in things that last. Will we? It's a good question for this stewardship season.

Looking at Katharine Drexel, another thought

comes to mind. She was able to accomplish as much as she did because of a strong spiritual foundation. She followed the example of her saintly parents, and the guidance of her spiritual director, and invested significant time and energy in worship and prayer. As a commentator put it, Katharine "had the deep realization that the (Christian) life must spring forth from the spirit of a contemplative prayer life or it would never produce good fruits."

Christ is the vine and we are the branches. If we stay connected with him, we can bear much fruit. But apart from him, we can do little or nothing. That's the gospel of John 9:9. Or, to refer to another of Jesus' parables, Katharine was like the wise man who built his house on a rock foundation, not sand, as in Matthew 7:24-27.

Her spirituality kept Katharine focused on what counts. It also made her humble. At age 84 she wrote, "Reflect on the (baby) Jesus. How tiny were his feet. We do not have to do anything too great in our lives: just follow those tiny footsteps. Then, let God do the rest and (God) will transform those tiny footsteps of ours into giant strides which will help us carry the peace, the hope, the love, and the joy which is Jesus Christ to all whom we meet."

Wise words from a wise woman! Reminds me of Mother Teresa, who said, famously, "In this life, we cannot do great things. We can only do small things with great love." Katharine Drexel offers us an example of saintly living and giving. She was rich, and became poor, for Christ's sake. That made her truly rich. But her greatest riches was her relationship with Christ. Katharine had discovered when you only have God,

God is more than enough, and all that you need. Katharine Drexel stored up her treasure in heaven. How do we measure our treasure? Are we investing our living and giving in things that last?

Saints Alive – Mother Teresa: "Saint Of The Gutters"

James 2.14-24.

All of us, I'm sure, know something about Mother Teresa. You probably know, for example, she won the Nobel Prize in 1979. You may know a poll placed her at the top of a list of the "most loved, most inspirational people of our age. Mother Teresa is ahead of Archbishop Desmond Tutu, Mahatma Gandhi, Martin Luther King Jr, and the Dalai Lama: quite an honor. Just two years after she died, Pope John Paul the Second put her on the fast track to sainthood, waiving the normal five year waiting period before consideration. Hers is the quickest beatification in modern times.

We know a lot about Mother Teresa, don't we? But she may be more complex than she seems. I'd like to tell her story as our "Saint of the Month." Mother Teresa has a lot to teach us, and not just about courage and compassion. She's also a great example of one who "kept on keeping on" in spite of nagging questions and doubts.

She was born Agnes Gonxh Bojaxhio (AG-ness GOHN-jay boh-yah-JOO) in present day Macedonia in 1910. That's my best effort at her native Albanian. She was the youngest child of a reasonably prosperous grocer, who died when she was eight. Agnes' mother was a devout Roman Catholic, a minority in her country. The girl was fascinated by stories of Roman Catholic missionaries to India. By age twelve Agnes was convinced her calling was to be a nun.

At eighteen she left her home and family forever. Agnes never saw her mother or sister again — total devotion. Instead she went to Ireland to learn English, so she could teach children in India, where English was the official language. She also learned Bengali, the language of the common people, on arriving in India.

She took her first vows as a nun and the religious name of Teresa, at age twenty. Then she spent seventeen years as an ordinary schoolteacher in the shadow of the Himalayas. Teresa loved teaching children and had a reasonably comfortable life. Her nights were spent behind the protective walls of a convent. Her days were spent in the schoolhouse next door.

Teresa was a good organizer. Her gifts were recognized early. By age 34 she was in charge of the convent. But the extreme poverty and suffering she saw around her continued to plague her. At age 36 she experienced what she called " a call within the call." Teresa came to believe she was, in her own words, ..."to leave the convent and help the poor while living among them. She said, "It was an order. To fail would have been to break the faith.[22]

Teresa left the comfortable convent and traded her nun's habit for a simple white cotton sari with a blue border, the traditional Indian dress. She got some rudimentary medical training, moved to the slums, and began to tend the destitute and dying, while herself living as the "poorest among the poor."

Her first year was terrible. She experienced doubt, loneliness, extreme poverty, and temptation to return to the convent. Teresa wrote in her diary, "The Lord wants me to be a free nun covered with the poverty of

---

[22] Joan Graff Clucas, *Mother Teresa* (New York: Chelsea House Publications, 1988), p. 35.

the Cross...Today...(w)hile looking for a home I walked and walked until my arms and legs ached. I thought how much (the poor) must ache in body and soul, looking for a home, food and health. Then the comfort of (my former convent) came to tempt me...'You have only to say the word and all will be yours again' the tempter kept on saying."[23]

But in spite of temptations to serve herself, not God, Teresa persisted. After three years she received permission to found a new order, The Missionaries of Charity. Their calling was to care for the hungry, the naked, the homeless, the crippled, the blind, the lepers, all those people who feel unwanted, unloved, uncared for throughout society, people who are shunned by everyone.[24] Eventually other like-minded women joined.

Her order started with thirteen members. Today they number more than four thousand nuns working at 610 missions plus many lay volunteers. In the 1960's a complimentary order of monks, the Missionaries of Charity Brothers, was added.

In 1953 Mother Teresa opened the first of her famous homes for the dying, in an abandoned Hindu Temple in Calcutta. There the destitute poor were allowed to die in dignity, each in accordance with his or her own faith. Muslims were treated like Muslims, Hindus like Hindus, and Christians like Christians. The goal was to offer a "beautiful death." So those who had "lived like animals" might "die like angels — loved and wanted."

Several years ago, while on a weekend retreat at the Spiritual Center in Maria Stein, Ohio, I met one of

---

23 Kathryn Spink, *Mother Teresa: A Complete Authorized Biography* (New York: HarperCollins, 1997), p. 31.

24 Brian Kolodiejchukm, *Mother Teresa: Come Be My Light* (New York: Doubleday, 2007), p. 187.

Mother Teresa's volunteers. When Susan Conroy was a young Dartmouth College graduate she worked with Mother Teresa twice in Calcutta. Conroy wrote a book about her experiences with this saint: *Mother Teresa's Lessons of Love and Secrets of Sanctity* (Huntington, IN: Our Sunday Visitor, Inc, 2003). She expected to experience hell on earth in India's slums. Instead, thanks to Mother Teresa, she discovered joy in the midst of suffering, peace in the face of chaos, and life in the midst of death. She reported the aged nun became a "true mother" to her.

Mother Teresa sought no attention for herself. Her ministry might be unknown, but for a British journalist. Malcolm Muggeridge was a devout Roman Catholic who first met her in 1968. This was more than two decades after she answered her calling within the calling in Calcutta.

Muggeridge was moved by her story, and popularized her through his bestseller, *Something Beautiful for God* (New York: HarperOne, 1986) As one commentator noted, "But for Malcolm Muggeridge, maybe even now no one would know her name. Mother Teresa would be just another faithful servant toiling away in God's vineyard, known only to God."

But the world did come to know her, and was moved by her example. Her stature allowed Mother Teresa to become a peacemaker worldwide. She ministered to Chernobyl survivors, the starving in Ethiopia, and earthquake victims in Armenia. She once entered a war zone to rescue 37 children caught in a crossfire between opposing forces.

Mother Teresa's caring and courage became more impressive, not less so, over time. At age 73 she suffered her first heart attack, ironically while visiting the

Pope. She had a second heart attack at at 79. This tiny woman (by the end of her life, she was only four foot ten) endured malaria and bouts of pneumonia. Observers watched her tend the dying not long before she herself died. The 87 year-old nun had a painful, broken collarbone, but still kept working! Nothing stopped Mother Teresa from her calling to live among the poorest of the poor for 51 years!

Poverty and pain were not the worst she endured. Believe it or not, Mother Teresa was frequently questioned and attacked. Like any prominent person, she had critics. An atheist author labeled her "Hell's Angel." Some liberal theologians found her "too Catholic." In fact her positions on divorce, abortion, and the Sacraments were ultra-conservative. But some fundamentalists felt Mother Teresa was too liberal! Instead of converting the dying to Christianity, if they were Muslim, she read them the Qu'ran; if they were Hindu, she read them the Vedas. These critics complained she wasn't a "true Christian" since she didn't preach Jesus as the one and only way to salvation. One critic complained she didn't quote the Bible enough! She was criticized for letting volunteers with limited medical training treat the sick and dying, although sometimes that's all she had.

Another charge was she took money from disreputable people. She in fact did receive a million and a half dollars from Charles Keating who was convicted of fraud. But that was before he was indicted. She took contributions from the Duvaliers, former dictators of Haiti, as well. Mother Teresa never spent money on herself. She gave even her Nobel prize money away. She was a good woman, and a great example. But even "saints" aren't perfect. Saints are people, and people aren't perfect. None of us are.

Still, her greatest challenge wasn't poverty, sickness, or criticism, but a crisis of faith. A recent book of her private diaries reveals Mother Teresa spent much of her later life plagued by doubt (see Brian Kolodiejchuk's *Mother Teresa: Come Be My Light*, New York: Doubleday, 2007). Her spiritual struggles lasted, off and on, for nearly fifty years. Like many saints before her, Mother Teresa was challenged in what was most essential. That was her faith.

She wrote, "Where is my faith? Even deep down... there is nothing but emptiness and darkness. When I try to raise my thoughts to heaven, there is such convincing emptiness that those thoughts return like sharp knives and hurt my very soul...Repulsed, empty, no faith, no love, no zeal...What do I labor for?"

Do you ever feel like that? If you have, you're in excellent company. Great Christians often have had to work through what Saint John of the Cross called "the dark night of the soul." Another Therese, Saint Therese of Lisieux, called it the "night of nothingness." Actually, Mother Teresa's persistence, in spite of doubts, makes her more impressive. She's a great example of one who "kept on keeping on" in spite of questions and doubts.

Ultimately her works are evidence of her faith. Listen to the letter of James: "What good is it, my brothers and sisters, if you say you have faith but do not have works? If a brother or sister is naked and lacks daily food, and one of you says to them, "Go in peace; keep warm and eat your fill," (in other words, 'Have a nice day'), and do not supply their bodily needs, what is the good of that? So faith, by itself, if it has no works, is dead..." He continues, "I by my works will show you my faith"(2:14-17, 18b, NRSV).

Mother Teresa saw her brothers and sisters in India lacked essentials, and supplied their needs. She did so not just out of humanitarian concern, but because Christ called her to do it. She even voluntarily accepted their poverty. That makes her a "type" of Christ who, out of love for us, joined us in our weakness by becoming human.

Mother Teresa herself said this, on accepting the Nobel Prize. "It is not enough for us to say, I love God, but I do not love my neighbor, since in dying on the cross, God had (made) himself the hungry one — the naked one — the homeless one."

Real faith results in real works. As a United Church of Christ bumper sticker puts it, "To believe is to care. To care is to do." Mother Teresa of Calcutta was one who, as the letter of James says, showed us her faith through her works. That's what makes her an inspiration — and a challenge — to all of us who call ourselves Christians.

Saints Alive – Nicholas of Myra: "An Advent Saint"

Isaiah 35:1-6, 9-10.

One thing I like about our new *Chalice Hymnal* is that it has a lot of Christmas music. There are about 55 Christmas carols in all. These songs lift up Jesus as "the reason for the Season" and help us put Christ back in Christmas. But aren't there lots of Santa Claus songs, too? These are tunes you hear in stores or on the radio this time of year. Favorites like "I Saw Mommy Kissing Santa Claus" (something I pondered as a child), "Up On The Housetop Reindeers Pause," "Rudolph, The Red-Nosed Reindeer," "Jolly Old Saint Nicholas," "Must Be Santa," that classic, "Grandma Got Run Over by a Reindeer," "Here Comes Santa Claus" or "Santa Claus is Coming to Town."

This time of year there's lots of emphasis on Santa. There is so much we might forget his origin as a Christian saint. It's his story I want to tell as our "saint of the month." Saint Nicholas is called "the Advent Saint" because his Saint's Day, December 6, comes early in Advent. Nicholas is an excellent example of faith, courage, and commitment in the Christian life.

I mentioned all the Santa songs we hear in this season. Turns out there are Saint Nicholas hymns as well — about twenty. They're sung mostly in Europe, where his feast day is a holiday. Some are quite lovely and are sung to familiar tunes, like "The Holly And The Ivy," "Angels, From The Realms Of Glory," "Jesus

Shall Reign Where'er The Sun" and even "The Battle Hymn Of The Republic!"

That last one seems odd, doesn't it? A battle hymn for a saint? Turns out jolly old Saint Nicholas could be combative. I'll explain that in a few minutes. Just so you'll know what these one of these hymns is like, I've added a Saint Nicholas carol this morning. We'll sing four hymns instead of three. The words are printed in your bulletins. The tune will be familiar.

Nicholas was born around 270 AD in the village of Patara. At the time the area was Greek and is now on the southern coast of Turkey. His wealthy parents were devout Christians, and raised their son as one. Unfortunately they both died in an epidemic when Nicholas was young. He was raised by his uncle, who was an abbot. Taking Jesus' words to the rich young ruler literally, "(G)o, sell what you own, and give the money to the poor, and you will have treasure in heaven" (Mark 10:21, NRSV), Nicholas set about giving his inheritance away. In the words of an ancient Greek hymn about him, "by poverty he gained wealth." His generous giving gave rise to Saint Nicholas' legends.

In one story a poor man lacked money for dowries for his three daughters. Without a dowry they were unlikely to find a husband. With no husband, poor as they were, they might end up as slaves. On learning this, Nicholas tossed three small bags of gold coins through the window at night. He did so secretly, to save the father's pride. Each bag was a dowry for one daughter. As the legend goes, the bags landed in socks the girls had hung on the mantle by the fire to dry. That's why children hang stockings by the fireplace on Christmas Eve. The incident tells us a lot about Nicholas' generous giving and also about the sensitivity and humility of this saint.

Nicholas tried to do what our lesson from Isaiah says. He sought to "(s)trenthen the weak hands...make firm the feeble knees." He said to the fearful of heart, "Be strong," do not fear, too. He sought to bring "joy and gladness" so "sorrow and sighing" would "flee away" (Isaiah 35.3-4a, 10b, NRSV). He was a good man, which his fellow Christians recognized early. They made him the Bishop of Myra, even though he hadn't first become a priest. This is attested to in several sources and was unusual. Nicholas served as bishop with courage and honor.

When he was in his early thirties, the emperor, Diocletian, launched a persecution of Christians. All church buildings were ordered destroyed. Every Christian book was to be burned. Many believers were tortured. Some were martyred. Many, like Bishop Nicholas, landed in jail. This persecution lasted, off and on, for ten years. But Saint Nicholas refused to deny his faith.

Eventually the emperor died and the firestorm ended. Nicholas was released. He went back to serving the church. Part of his duties included traveling from parish to parish. Maybe this is where the idea of Santa as a traveler started. Saint Nicholas didn't have reindeer and a sleigh. But he did have adventures. On one occasion, according to legend, he calmed a storm that was sinking his ship. That made him the patron saint of sailors and got his name and fame spread throughout the world. Everywhere seafarers went they built chapels to Saint Nicholas. Another time, according to legend, he saved three children. So St. Nicholas came to be recognized as the patron saint of children, too. This has an obvious connection to today's Santa Claus.

But it's his giving, like the gift of dowries for three daughters, that captured Christians' imaginations. As far back as the Middle Ages, nuns used to celebrate his Saint's Day, December 6, by depositing baskets of food and clothing on the doorsteps of the poor. Much gift giving by believers around Christmas is in the spirit of St. Nicholas. In fact, in the United States, 30% of all gifts to charity are made in December. We give because we first have received, blessing upon blessing, through God's Son.

Nicholas wasn't only a gift giver — like some holly, jolly Santa. He also was a fierce defender of the faith. He attended the Nicaea Council in 325 CE — the first great, worldwide council of the church. The theological debates got hot and thick. Nicholas was outraged by the heretic Arius, who contended Christ was not fully divine. They fell to blows. In the process, according to the story, Nicholas hit Arius, knocking him down and breaking his nose. Saint Nicholas could be something of a scrapper, too, in pursuit of a righteous cause!

In spite of his persecution, imprisonment, adventures, and occasional fighting, Nicholas had a rich, full life. He lived to the age of nearly eighty. After he died, his body was preserved. Originally it rested in his hometown of Patara. But around 1,100 sailors moved his body, when his homeland was conquered by Muslims. They wanted to protect Nicholas as he protected them. Remember, he's the patron saint of sailors.

They took him to Bari, Italy, where his bones now rest. What's unusual about Saint Nicholas is his remains are almost all there. Saints often got divided up in Medieval times, an elaborately decorated bone chip here, a scrap of hair there. For example, at the National

Marian Shrine of the Holy Relics at Maria Stein, Ohio, they display relics of almost 1,000 saints, but not very much of any one, often just a chip of bone. But Saint Nicholas's remains are more complete. With the Pope's permission, scientists have studied Nicholas. They discovered he was barely five feet tall: shorter than average. Ironically, Nicholas himself also had a broken nose!

Seventeen hundred years after he lived, Nicholas of Myra is recognized worldwide. For example, he's a favored saint in Albania. Albanians swear oaths by saying, "May I see holy Saint Nicholas." They celebrate his day, December 6th, with a feast. On the eve of his feast they abstain from meat and light a candle, but also prepare roast lamb and pork. At the start of the new day, they greet each other with, "May the night of Saint Nicholas help you." Then they sit down to a huge midnight meal. It's a custom Mother Teresa, who grew up in Albania, would have known.

Of course, in America, Saint Nicholas has morphed into Santa. This trend is growing worldwide. Several years ago, in his birthplace, the mayor replaced a beautiful bronze statue of a solemn Saint Nicholas with a giant, red-suited plastic Santa. The traditional Saint Nicholas was pushed into a corner. The mayor wanted a Saint Nicholas tourists would recognize. In spite of this trend, we need not push this saint aside!

As I said, there are many St. Nicholas hymns. I'll introduce you to one. It's "Good St. Nicholas of Myra, written by J. M. Rosenthal in 1999. It can be sung to the familiar tune Regent Square, or *Angels, from the Realms of Glory*:

Good St. Nicholas of Myra[25]
deeds and legends tell his fame.
Saintly bishop, friend of children
Bari pilgrims chant the name:
Bless'd Nicholas, Bless'd Nicholas
He loved all in Jesus' name.

Miracles and signs and wonders
he performed to praise the Lord.
For a poor and weary people
source of care and joy out poured:
Bless'd Nicholas, Bless'd Nicholas
He loved all in Jesus' name.

Sailors, nations, people thank him
for the message that he brought.
Young and old now hail the memory
Of the lessons that he taught:
Bless'd Nicholas, Bless'd Nicholas
He loved all in Jesus' name.

May his ways of true devotion
guide us on our earthly way.
Challenge us to be more like him
as Christ's gospel we obey:
Bless'd Nicholas, Bless'd Nicholas
He loved all in Jesus' name.

Father, Son and Holy Spirit
bind us in community,
so that we with holy Nicholas
might eternal glory see:
Bless'd Nicholas, Bless'd Nicholas
He loved all in Jesus' name.

---

25 Pronounced like the woman's name.

That fourth verse is a good thought to end on, as we think of the meaning of Christmas and the saint behind Santa: May (Saint Nicholas') ways of true devotion guide us on our earthly way. Challenge us to be more like him, as Christ's gospel we obey. Bless'd Nicholas, Bless'd Nicholas (May *we* love)all in Jesus' name. Santa Claus may have lots of gifts to bring us. But Saint Nicholas gifts us, too, with his example of faith, courage, and commitment in the Christian life.

Saints Alive – You and I: "Called To Be Saints"

1 Corinthians 1:1-9.

This year I have preached a series on saints of the church. They were men and women who led extraordinary Christian lives. Saint Patrick, Saint Francis, Father Damien, the leper priest of Molokai and Mother Teresa of Calcutta were some of the great Christians we considered. Also Katherine Drexel, who gave up one of the largest fortunes in America to become a nun.

Most of us would agree with the saintliness of Francis of Assisi, Father Damien, or Mother Teresa. But what about the Corinthians? Saint Paul's letter to the Church at Corinth reveals a deeply divided and terribly troubled group. This congregation was beset by almost every conceivable weakness and sin.

We learn from reading First Corinthians (1:12) that the church was split into angry factions. Its members were full of conceit (4:8). They tolerated sexual immorality (5:1), patronized prostitutes (6:15), toyed with idolatry (10:14), turned their worship services into circuses (12:33), got drunk at the Lord's Supper (11:21), and sued each other in court (6:1).

But Saint Paul calls the Corinthians "saints." First Corinthians 1:2 says, "To the church of God that is in Corinth, to those who are sanctified (that is, made saints) in Christ Jesus, called to be saints" (NRSV). He also says they are not lacking in any spiritual gifts!

The confused Corinthians in the same category as Father Damien and Mother Teresa? What's going on here? Paul obviously sees the Corinthians with bifocal glasses. With one lens he sees them as they currently are. Paul is under no illusions about the state of this church. In fact he chides them and corrects them for much of this letter.

But with the other lens he sees them as they are called to be, and could be, through the grace of God. Truth be told, most Christians and most congregations need the same, double-lens viewing. Yes, we may give in to sin, but we're also called saints and called to be saints.

In New Testament Greek, the word "saint" is simply another word for "believer." In the Greek, "saint" is "hagio" which can be translated "separated," "dedicated" or "set aside." Under this definition, the Corinthians, and each of us, is a saint. That's right, a saint! Because each of us has been set aside by God. God has chosen us and set us apart for three purposes, all of which are mentioned in 1 Corinthians. We are called to be sinless. We are called to spread the word. We are called to serve. We are set apart from the rest of the world for these three tasks, according to Paul.

First, as saints, we are called to be sinless. That's God's ultimate goal for you and me. We are to become, in the prophet Isaiah's picturesque term, "a light to the nations" (49:6). Kings and princes, promises the prophet, will bow down before us. We will be perfect in every way.

Of course, the more sensitive among us are quite aware of our current imperfections. We know we fail to meet God's high standards every day. We're quite unlike Rabbi Simeon ben Jochai, an actual historical figure. He once declared, "If there are only two righteous men in the world, I and my son are these two. If there is only one righteous man alive, I am he." Or the overbearing husbands alluded to in a T-shirt I once saw, a T-shirt worn by a long-suffering wife. The T-shirt read, "I married Mr. Right. I just didn't know his first name was Always."

No, most of us know we are far from always right, or always sinless. But God is very giving and very patient, and has eternity to work on us and with us. As C. S. Lewis, author of *The Chronicles of Narnia* put it, "The command 'Be... perfect' is not idealistic gas. Nor is it a command to do the impossible. (God) is going to make us into creatures that can obey that command. He said (in the Bible) that we were 'gods' and he is going to make good his words. If we let him — for we can prevent him, if we choose — he will make the feeblest and filthiest of us into a god or goddess, dazzling radiant, immortal creatures, pulsating all through with such energy and joy and wisdom and love as we cannot now imagine, a bright stainless mirror which reflects back to him perfectly (though on a smaller scale). His own boundless power and delight and goodness. The process (which theologians call 'sanctification') will be long and in parts very painful; but that is what we are in for. Nothing less. (God) meant what he said."[26]

We've got to be patient with ourselves, because God isn't done with us yet. Every one of us is a faultless, flawless creation *under construction*. It may take a thousand million years for God to get all the bugs and blemishes out of you or me. But God is patient. God

---
26   C. S. Lewis, *Mere Christianity*, (New York: Macmillan, 1952, p. 174.

will do it, if we allow it. After all, God has all the time in the world!

So we also need to be patient with each other. Just as you and I are *under construction*, so are those other saints who irritate or annoy us from time to time. We might like them better, and tolerate them more, if we could focus on their potential, and not their present failings. As saints, we are called to be sinless, and to be a light to the world.

Secondly, as saints, we are called to spread the gospel. Just as we need to hear about God's forgiveness and plan for our perfection, so others outside the church need to hear that word. I'm reminded of the story about a little boy who was brought to a beautiful Roman Catholic church by his mother. That church was graced with many stunning stained glass windows. Many of the windows were dedicated to saints.

Mother pointed them out: Saint Anthony, Saint Aloyscius, Saint Agnes, etc. But the boy was puzzled. "What's a saint?" he asked. Mother thought for a moment, then replied, "A saint is someone who lets the light shine through!" It's unlikely any of us will be pictured on a stained-glass window. Still, when we share our faith, God's light shines through. In so doing, we give the gift that keeps on giving: the opportunity for someone to begin a new relationship with God.

I think of some of the "saints" who have helped me on my spiritual journey. They include my parents — especially my mother — who taught me my first lessons about God, the Bible, and prayer. There was my long-time pastor in our hometown who was a freedom marcher for civil rights in the South in the 1960's. He gave me an early example of devotion and helped guide me to ordination.

There was a college professor of religion whose radiant life was evidence of the joy of following Christ. There were two seminary students who led me to a born-again experience. These folks were saints in my life. All of them witnessed to me in a way that helped change me for the better.

Maybe you or I can equally be a saint to another person. What could be more lasting than bringing another to God? It's great to build a business, but someday someone else will own it. It's an accomplishment to buy a house, but it eventually will end up in someone else's hands. It's an achievement to earn a Ph.D. But, with time, even the greatest scholars can be forgotten.

What we accomplish spiritually is what ultimately lasts. D. L. Moody, the great nineteenth century evangelist from our Congregationalist tradition wrote, "The monument I want after I am dead is a monument with two legs going around the world: a saved sinner telling about the salvation of Jesus Christ." As saints, we're called to witness to the gospel, to let the light shine through. In so doing we make an important contribution to others lives, and to the life of the world.

Finally, as saints, we are to provide Christian service. As an old hymn puts it, "Where cross the crowded ways of life, where sound the cries of race and clan... in haunts of wretchedness and need, on shadowed thresholds dark with fears," we are to be carriers of God's love.

We are to feed the hungry, give drink to the thirsty, welcome the stranger, help clothe the naked, and visit the sick and the prisoner (Matthew 25:31-46). Since Jesus no longer walks among us, in doing those things, we are to be his hands and feet.

That might sound like an overwhelming challenge. Some of us may not feel up to it. Maybe we can't all do great things, but we all can do small things with great love, as the late Mother Teresa put it. In God's eyes, even small things become great if they are driven by love.

Consider the story of SARA, (Sharing America's Resources Abroad). Let me tell you how this Ohio-based, volunteer-run organization began. The Reverend Steve Szilagyi, a United Church of Christ pastor from Ohio was visiting his homeland of Hungary. While driving through a village, he noticed a boy crippled by scoliosis. Steve's heart went out to the child. In fact, he prayed for him, that the boy's life might get better. Steve and his wife were heading somewhere else, and did not stop.

But his wife was feeling ill. Actually she needed the restroom. So they turned back to the town. There was the crippled boy again. Steve took this as a sign he was not just to pray but to do something to help him. He met the boy and his family, returned to the States and raised enough money to bring the boy here for successful surgery, which couldn't have been done at that time in Hungary.

It didn't take long for Steve to figure out there were lots of kids in Hungary with scoliosis. He found that the best way to treat them was not to bring each one to the US but to train doctors here and send them back to Europe. SARA, (Sharing America's Resources Abroad), was born. Since then, SARA has provided around twenty million dollars of medical equipment and training to clinics, hospitals, and doctors in ten countries. All this because an Ohio UCC pastor cared enough to pray for and help a little boy.

Martin Luther King Jr. didn't start out to reform racial justice all over America. He began by organizing a one-day bus boycott in Montgomery, Alabama, a mid-size city. His immediate concern was a $14.00 fine unjustly levied against Rosa Parks. King did small things with great courage. Who among us, like Steve Szilagyi, or Dr. King or Mother Teresa, will hear God's call to service and say, "Here I am." Mother Teresa wrote, "We must not drift away from humble works, because these are the works nobody will do. It's never too small. We are so small we look at things in a small way. But God, being almighty, sees everything great."

She continued, "Therefore, even if you write a letter for a blind man or you just go and sit and listen, or you take the mail for him, or you visit somebody or bring a flower to somebody---small things--or wash clothes for somebody or clean the house. Very humble work... is where you and I must be. For there are many people who can do big things. But there are very few people who will do the small."[27]

That woman was a saint! But so are we! Like the Corinthians, we are called to be sinless, we are called to spread the gospel, we are called to service. We're saints. If we accept our calling, there's no limit to what God might do through us.

---

27 http://www.compassioninstitute.com

www.ingramcontent.com/pod-product-compliance
Lightning Source LLC
Chambersburg PA
CBHW071728040426
42446CB00011B/2267